I0008104

Federated Identity and Single Sign-On

James Relington

Copyright © 2025 James Relington

All rights reserved

DEDICATION

To all cybersecurity professionals. Your commitment to protecting access, enforcing governance, and navigating the complexities of identity management is invaluable. May this work serve as a guide and inspiration in your ongoing efforts to create a more secure and compliant future.

Introduction to Federated Identity and SSO 8

The Evolution of Identity Management...10

Key Concepts in Identity and Access Management (IAM) 13

Authentication vs. Authorization: Understanding the Difference 17

The Role of Identity Providers (IdPs) and Service Providers (SPs).....20

Identity Federation Models and Use Cases 23

Security Considerations in Identity Management................................27

The Basics of SAML (Security Assertion Markup Language) 30

OAuth 2.0: Delegated Authorization for Applications 34

OpenID Connect: Authentication on Top of OAuth 2.0......................37

JWTs (JSON Web Tokens) and Their Role in SSO...............................41

Kerberos Authentication and Single Sign-On 44

LDAP and Active Directory in Identity Management.........................48

Passwordless Authentication: The Future of SSO 52

How Federated Identity Works: A Technical Overview 55

Setting Up an Identity Provider (IdP) 59

Configuring a Service Provider (SP) for Federation 63

Federation Metadata: What It Is and Why It Matters 67

Implementing SAML-Based SSO in an Enterprise Environment.........71

Integrating OAuth 2.0 and OpenID Connect in Web Applications....75

User Provisioning and Deprovisioning in Federated Identity.............79

Attribute Mapping and Claims Transformation................................82

Identity Governance and Compliance in Federated Identity.............86

Common Security Risks in Federated Identity...................................90

Protecting Against Man-in-the-Middle (MITM) Attacks in SSO........94

Token Hijacking and Replay Attacks: Prevention Strategies 98

Securing Identity Federation with Certificate Management 101

Managing Session Security and Token Expiry in SSO 105

Zero Trust and Its Relationship with Federated Identity...................109

Federation in Multi-Cloud and Hybrid Cloud Environments............113

Identity Federation in Government and Healthcare Sectors 117

Role-Based Access Control (RBAC) and Attribute-Based Access Control (ABAC)..121

Integrating SSO with Mobile and IoT Devices 124

Cross-Domain Identity Federation: Challenges and Solutions 128

Leveraging AI and Machine Learning in Identity Management 132

Decentralized Identity and Self-Sovereign Identity (SSI) 135

Using Microsoft Entra ID (Azure AD) for Federated Identity...........139

AKNOWLEDGEMENTS

I extend my deepest gratitude to everyone who contributed to the creation of this book. To my colleagues and mentors in the field of identity governance, your insights and expertise have been invaluable. To my friends and family, your unwavering support and encouragement have made this journey possible. To the professionals and innovators dedicated to securing digital identities, your work continues to inspire and shape the future of cybersecurity. This book is a reflection of collective knowledge, and I am grateful to all who have played a role in its development.

Introduction to Federated Identity and SSO

In today's digital landscape, managing user identities and access across multiple applications and services has become a critical challenge for organizations. As businesses adopt cloud-based services, mobile applications, and third-party integrations, the need for a seamless, secure, and efficient authentication system has grown exponentially. Federated identity and Single Sign-On (SSO) have emerged as essential solutions to streamline user authentication, enhance security, and improve the overall user experience.

Federated identity refers to a system in which a user's identity is managed across multiple organizations or service providers without requiring separate credentials for each one. This approach enables users to authenticate once and gain access to multiple applications without needing to repeatedly enter their credentials. Instead of each application maintaining its own user database, identity verification is delegated to a central identity provider (IdP), which issues authentication tokens that can be trusted by other services. This reduces the administrative burden of managing multiple user accounts and passwords while also minimizing security risks associated with credential management.

Single Sign-On (SSO) is a key component of federated identity that allows users to log in once and gain access to multiple systems without needing to re-enter their credentials. With SSO, users can authenticate with an identity provider, which then issues session tokens or security assertions that grant access to various applications. This process improves convenience for users while reducing password fatigue, which is a common issue when users are required to manage numerous passwords across different platforms. SSO can be implemented using various authentication protocols, such as SAML (Security Assertion Markup Language), OAuth 2.0, and OpenID Connect. These protocols define how authentication and authorization information is exchanged between identity providers and service providers.

The benefits of federated identity and SSO extend beyond user convenience. Security is a major advantage, as centralized authentication reduces the risks associated with weak or reused passwords. Users are less likely to use simple or easily guessable passwords when they only need to remember a single set of credentials. Additionally, federated identity allows organizations to enforce stronger authentication mechanisms, such as multi-factor authentication (MFA), without requiring separate implementations for each application. This ensures a higher level of security while simplifying the user experience.

Organizations also benefit from improved efficiency and cost savings. Managing user accounts across multiple applications can be complex and resource-intensive, especially in large enterprises with thousands of users. Federated identity reduces the need for redundant account management tasks, such as resetting passwords, provisioning new accounts, and deactivating inactive users. By centralizing identity management, IT teams can focus on more strategic security initiatives rather than spending time on routine administrative tasks. Moreover, federated identity supports regulatory compliance by providing a standardized way to manage user access and authentication. Regulations such as GDPR, HIPAA, and SOC 2 require organizations to implement strict controls over user access to sensitive data. Federated identity simplifies compliance by offering audit trails, centralized access controls, and the ability to revoke access instantly when necessary.

Despite its benefits, implementing federated identity and SSO comes with challenges. One of the primary concerns is trust between identity providers and service providers. Organizations must establish strong trust relationships to ensure that authentication assertions are reliable and secure. Additionally, integrating different authentication protocols across various systems can be complex, especially when dealing with legacy applications that do not support modern standards. Security risks also exist, particularly if the identity provider itself becomes compromised. Because federated identity centralizes authentication, a breach of the identity provider could potentially expose multiple services to unauthorized access. To mitigate this risk, organizations must implement strong security controls, such as encryption, token expiration policies, and continuous monitoring for suspicious activities.

Another challenge is user adoption. While federated identity simplifies authentication, users may need to adjust to new login methods or multi-factor authentication requirements. Educating users on the benefits of SSO and providing clear guidance on how to use it effectively can help reduce friction during the transition. Organizations must also consider scenarios where external partners or third-party users need access to their systems. Federated identity solutions should be flexible enough to accommodate various user groups while maintaining strict access control policies.

As technology continues to evolve, the role of federated identity and SSO is becoming increasingly important. The rise of cloud computing, mobile applications, and remote work has accelerated the need for secure and efficient authentication mechanisms. Organizations that adopt federated identity can enhance security, reduce administrative complexity, and improve user experience, making it a fundamental component of modern identity and access management strategies.

The Evolution of Identity Management

The concept of identity management has undergone significant transformations over the years, adapting to the ever-changing landscape of technology, security threats, and user expectations. In the early days of computing, identity management was a simple, localized process where user credentials were stored on individual systems. As organizations expanded and networks grew, the need for more sophisticated authentication and access control mechanisms became evident. This evolution has led to the development of centralized directories, federated identity systems, and modern cloud-based identity solutions that are now fundamental to securing digital interactions.

In the earliest stages of computing, identity management was rudimentary. Users would log into standalone systems using a username and password, with credentials stored directly on the local machine. There was no need for complex identity verification since most systems were isolated and only accessible to a limited number of users. However, as businesses started networking their systems together, the need for a more scalable approach emerged. Organizations required a way to authenticate users across multiple machines without forcing them to remember numerous credentials. This led to the introduction of centralized authentication systems, such as UNIX-based authentication models and early directory services.

The advent of enterprise networks in the late 20th century brought new challenges. Businesses needed a way to manage user access across multiple applications, which led to the development of directory services such as the Lightweight Directory Access Protocol (LDAP) and Microsoft's Active Directory. These systems allowed organizations to centralize user identities, enabling employees to log into different services using a single set of credentials. This was a significant improvement over isolated authentication models, as it reduced administrative overhead and improved security by allowing centralized control over user accounts and permissions.

As organizations grew more complex, so did their IT environments. Companies began integrating multiple applications, each with its own authentication mechanism, leading to the problem of "password fatigue." Users were required to remember numerous usernames and passwords, often resorting to insecure practices such as reusing passwords or writing them down. To address this, Single Sign-On (SSO) solutions were introduced, allowing users to authenticate once and gain access to multiple services without needing to re-enter their credentials. Early SSO implementations were primarily used within corporate intranets, relying on protocols such as Kerberos and NTLM for authentication.

The rise of the internet and web applications in the early 2000s further changed the landscape of identity management. Organizations needed to authenticate users not only within their internal networks but also for externally hosted services and cloud applications. This shift led to the adoption of federated identity management, a model in which users could authenticate with a trusted identity provider and access multiple third-party services without needing separate accounts. Technologies such as Security Assertion Markup Language (SAML) and later OAuth 2.0 and OpenID Connect enabled secure authentication and authorization across different domains.

With the widespread adoption of cloud computing, identity management evolved even further. Traditional on-premises directory services were no longer sufficient to manage access to cloud-based applications and services. This gave rise to Identity as a Service (IDaaS) solutions, such as Microsoft Entra ID (formerly Azure AD), Okta, and Google Workspace Identity. These cloud-based identity providers offered seamless authentication across both on-premises and cloud environments, enabling businesses to maintain a unified identity infrastructure while supporting remote work and mobile access.

Security concerns have always played a critical role in shaping the evolution of identity management. As cyber threats became more sophisticated, organizations realized that relying solely on passwords was not enough to protect user identities. Multi-Factor Authentication (MFA) emerged as a necessary enhancement, requiring users to verify their identity using multiple factors such as something they know (password), something they have (a mobile device or security key), or something they are (biometric authentication). This additional layer of security significantly reduced the risk of unauthorized access, even if passwords were compromised.

The evolution of identity management also saw the rise of role-based access control (RBAC) and attribute-based access control (ABAC). Instead of granting users broad access to systems, organizations started implementing fine-grained access controls based on job roles, responsibilities, and contextual factors. These models improved security by ensuring that users only had access to the resources necessary for their work, reducing the risk of insider threats and accidental data breaches.

More recently, the concept of Zero Trust has further influenced identity management strategies. Traditional security models relied on the assumption that users inside a corporate network could be trusted, while those outside required stricter authentication. However, with the increase in remote work, cloud services, and mobile devices, this model became obsolete. Zero Trust assumes that no user or device should be trusted by default, requiring continuous verification and real-time risk assessment before granting access to resources. This shift has led to the adoption of adaptive authentication, where identity verification methods dynamically adjust based on factors such as user behavior, location, and device security posture.

The next phase in identity management is expected to focus on decentralized identity and passwordless authentication. Decentralized identity leverages blockchain and self-sovereign identity (SSI) principles to give users greater control over their personal data, allowing them to authenticate without relying on a central authority. Meanwhile, passwordless authentication methods, such as biometric authentication, security keys, and passkeys, are gaining traction as organizations seek to eliminate password-related vulnerabilities altogether.

Identity management has come a long way from its early days of standalone credentials to today's sophisticated, cloud-based, and AI-driven authentication models. As technology continues to advance, the focus will remain on improving security, reducing friction for users, and enabling seamless access to digital services while mitigating risks associated with identity theft and cyber threats.

Key Concepts in Identity and Access Management (IAM)

Identity and Access Management (IAM) is a fundamental aspect of modern cybersecurity and IT infrastructure, ensuring that users and systems have appropriate access to resources while maintaining security and compliance. As organizations continue to expand their digital ecosystems, managing identities effectively becomes more complex and crucial. IAM encompasses various principles, technologies, and practices designed to control and monitor access to applications, data, and networks. Understanding the key concepts in IAM is essential for securing sensitive information, preventing unauthorized access, and enhancing operational efficiency.

At the core of IAM is the concept of identity, which refers to the unique representation of an individual, system, or device within an organization's network. Each identity is associated with attributes such as username, email, department, job role, and authentication credentials. These attributes help define who or what is accessing a system and determine the appropriate level of access. Unlike traditional user management, IAM goes beyond just usernames and passwords by integrating multiple authentication methods, identity verification processes, and access control mechanisms.

Authentication is a critical component of IAM, responsible for verifying that a user or system is who they claim to be. Traditional authentication methods rely on passwords, but due to the increasing risks associated with password-based security, organizations are shifting towards more robust authentication mechanisms. Multi-Factor Authentication (MFA) enhances security by requiring users to provide additional verification factors, such as a one-time code sent to their mobile device, biometric data, or hardware security tokens. This approach significantly reduces the likelihood of unauthorized access, even if a password is compromised.

Authorization is another essential aspect of IAM, determining what an authenticated user can do within a system. It ensures that users only have access to the resources necessary for their job functions and prevents excessive privileges that could lead to security breaches. Role-Based Access Control (RBAC) is a widely used authorization model that assigns permissions based on predefined roles within an organization. For example, an employee in the HR department may have access to personnel records but not to financial systems. Attribute-Based Access Control (ABAC) extends this concept by using attributes such as location, device type, or time of access to dynamically enforce access policies.

The principle of least privilege (PoLP) is a fundamental security best practice in IAM. It dictates that users should be granted the minimum level of access required to perform their tasks. By limiting unnecessary permissions, organizations reduce the risk of insider threats, accidental data exposure, and privilege escalation attacks. Implementing least privilege requires continuous monitoring of user activities and regularly reviewing access rights to ensure they align with current job responsibilities.

Identity federation plays a significant role in IAM by enabling users to authenticate once and gain access to multiple applications across different organizations or domains. This concept is particularly useful in environments where employees, partners, and customers need seamless access to various services without managing multiple credentials. Federated identity relies on trust relationships between identity providers (IdPs) and service providers (SPs), allowing authentication credentials to be shared securely. Technologies such as Security Assertion Markup Language (SAML), OAuth 2.0, and OpenID Connect facilitate identity federation and enable Single Sign-On (SSO) capabilities.

Single Sign-On (SSO) is a user-friendly authentication approach that allows individuals to log in once and access multiple systems without repeatedly entering credentials. By reducing password fatigue and minimizing the risks associated with weak or reused passwords, SSO enhances both security and user experience. However, SSO must be implemented carefully to avoid creating a single point of failure. Strong authentication and session management practices are necessary to ensure that an attacker compromising one account does not gain access to all associated services.

Identity lifecycle management is another critical concept in IAM, focusing on the processes involved in creating, maintaining, and deactivating identities. This lifecycle begins when a user is onboarded into an organization, requiring the creation of an identity with appropriate access rights. Throughout the user's tenure, access needs may change due to role transitions, promotions, or department transfers. IAM solutions must facilitate automated provisioning and deprovisioning of accounts to ensure that access rights remain aligned with business requirements. When a user leaves the organization, timely deactivation of accounts is essential to prevent unauthorized access.

Privileged Access Management (PAM) is a specialized subset of IAM that focuses on securing accounts with elevated permissions, such as system administrators, database managers, and executives with access to sensitive information. Privileged accounts are high-value targets for cyber attackers, as they provide extensive control over IT systems. PAM solutions enforce strict access controls, monitor privileged user activities, and implement just-in-time access mechanisms to minimize exposure to security risks.

Auditability and compliance are integral aspects of IAM, ensuring that organizations meet regulatory requirements and maintain visibility into user activities. Security frameworks such as GDPR, HIPAA, and SOC 2 mandate stringent identity management practices, including access logging, user activity monitoring, and periodic access reviews. IAM systems generate audit trails that help organizations detect anomalies, investigate security incidents, and demonstrate compliance during regulatory audits.

Adaptive authentication is an emerging concept in IAM that enhances security by dynamically adjusting authentication requirements based on contextual factors. Instead of applying a one-size-fits-all approach, adaptive authentication evaluates risk signals such as login location, device health, and user behavior to determine the appropriate level of authentication. For example, a user logging in from an unfamiliar location may be required to complete an additional verification step, while a login from a trusted device in a usual location may proceed seamlessly. This risk-based approach improves security without unnecessarily burdening users with frequent authentication challenges.

The integration of artificial intelligence and machine learning into IAM is transforming how organizations manage identities and detect security threats. AI-driven IAM solutions analyze user behavior patterns, identify anomalies, and predict potential security risks. By leveraging machine learning algorithms, IAM systems can detect fraudulent activities, automate access decision-making, and enhance threat response capabilities. This proactive approach helps organizations stay ahead of evolving cyber threats and strengthen their identity security posture.

As digital transformation accelerates, the importance of IAM continues to grow. Organizations must adopt robust identity management strategies to protect sensitive data, prevent unauthorized access, and ensure compliance with security regulations. By understanding and implementing key IAM concepts, businesses can create a secure and efficient access control framework that supports both operational needs and cybersecurity requirements.

Authentication vs. Authorization: Understanding the Difference

In the realm of cybersecurity and identity management, two fundamental concepts govern access control: authentication and authorization. While often used interchangeably, they serve distinct purposes in ensuring secure access to systems, applications, and data. Authentication is the process of verifying a user's identity, while authorization determines what an authenticated user is allowed to do. Understanding the distinction between these concepts is essential for implementing robust security policies and preventing unauthorized access to sensitive resources.

Authentication is the first step in any access control process. It answers the question, "Who are you?" by requiring users to prove their identity before gaining access to a system. Traditionally, authentication relied on usernames and passwords, but due to the increasing risks associated with password-based security, additional methods have been developed. Multi-Factor Authentication (MFA) enhances security by requiring users to provide multiple forms of verification, such as a password (something they know), a fingerprint scan (something they are), or a security token (something they have). Biometric authentication, such as facial recognition and fingerprint scanning, has also become a common method for verifying identity, particularly in mobile and enterprise environments.

A well-implemented authentication mechanism ensures that only legitimate users gain access to a system. However, authentication alone does not determine what actions a user can perform once they are logged in. This is where authorization comes into play. Authorization answers the question, "What are you allowed to do?" Even if a user successfully authenticates, they must still have the appropriate permissions to access specific resources or perform certain actions.

Authorization controls define what a user can view, modify, or execute within an application or network.

A common analogy to illustrate the difference between authentication and authorization is the process of entering a hotel. When a guest arrives at the front desk, they are required to present identification and a reservation confirmation to verify their identity—this step represents authentication. Once their identity is confirmed, the hotel assigns them a room key, which grants access to their specific room but not to other guests' rooms, staff-only areas, or maintenance facilities. This access restriction is the equivalent of authorization, as it ensures that the guest can only access the resources they are permitted to use.

In enterprise environments, authentication and authorization are managed using identity and access management (IAM) solutions that enforce security policies across applications and systems. Authentication mechanisms such as Single Sign-On (SSO) allow users to authenticate once and gain access to multiple services without repeatedly entering credentials. SSO enhances user convenience while reducing the risk of password-related security breaches. However, SSO only addresses authentication; organizations must still implement proper authorization controls to enforce role-based access policies and prevent users from accessing data they are not authorized to view.

Role-Based Access Control (RBAC) and Attribute-Based Access Control (ABAC) are common authorization models used to enforce security policies. In an RBAC model, users are assigned roles based on their job functions, and each role has predefined permissions. For example, an employee in the finance department may have access to accounting software but not to HR records. ABAC extends this concept by evaluating additional attributes, such as user location, time of access, or device type, to make dynamic access decisions. These authorization models ensure that users receive the appropriate level of access based on business requirements and security policies.

A significant security risk arises when authentication is strong but authorization is poorly implemented. If a system correctly verifies a user's identity but fails to restrict access based on permissions, it can lead to data breaches and privilege escalation attacks. A classic example of weak authorization is the failure to enforce least privilege access. If an employee in the marketing department gains administrative access to financial records due to misconfigured permissions, it creates a security vulnerability that could be exploited. Organizations must conduct regular access reviews and enforce strict authorization policies to mitigate these risks.

Conversely, overly restrictive authorization policies can hinder productivity. If users lack the necessary permissions to perform their job functions, they may resort to insecure workarounds, such as sharing credentials or using unauthorized applications. Striking the right balance between security and usability is crucial when designing authentication and authorization frameworks. Implementing Just-in-Time (JIT) access and Privileged Access Management (PAM) solutions can help organizations grant temporary elevated permissions when needed while ensuring that access is revoked once the task is completed.

Another critical aspect of authentication and authorization is session management. Once a user is authenticated, the system must maintain their session securely while preventing unauthorized access. Session tokens, cookies, and access tokens are used to maintain authentication states across multiple requests. However, if session tokens are not properly secured, attackers can hijack them to gain unauthorized access. Implementing session timeouts, token expiration policies, and secure storage mechanisms is essential for preventing session-based attacks.

Modern authentication and authorization frameworks leverage federated identity systems to enable seamless access across multiple platforms and organizations. Federated authentication allows users to log in using credentials from a trusted identity provider, such as Google, Microsoft, or an enterprise directory service. This approach simplifies user management while enhancing security through centralized authentication policies. Once a user is authenticated through a federated identity provider, service providers can enforce authorization policies based on predefined access control rules.

As cyber threats continue to evolve, organizations must continuously refine their authentication and authorization strategies. Implementing adaptive authentication, which dynamically adjusts authentication requirements based on risk factors, enhances security without creating unnecessary friction for users. Similarly, continuous authorization monitoring ensures that access policies remain aligned with business needs and security best practices. By integrating authentication and authorization into a comprehensive IAM strategy, organizations can protect sensitive data, prevent unauthorized access, and ensure compliance with regulatory requirements.

The Role of Identity Providers (IdPs) and Service Providers (SPs)

In modern identity and access management (IAM), two essential components define how authentication and authorization processes function across different systems: Identity Providers (IdPs) and Service Providers (SPs). These two entities work together to enable seamless access to digital services while maintaining security and reducing the burden of managing multiple credentials. Understanding their roles, how they interact, and their importance in federated identity management is crucial for organizations looking to implement secure and efficient authentication mechanisms.

An Identity Provider (IdP) is an entity responsible for verifying user identities and issuing authentication tokens or assertions that other systems can trust. IdPs act as the authoritative source of identity data, storing user credentials, attributes, and authentication policies. They play a crucial role in federated authentication, allowing users to authenticate once with the IdP and then access multiple services without needing to log in again. Examples of well-known IdPs include Microsoft Entra ID (formerly Azure AD), Okta, Google Workspace, and Ping Identity. These platforms centralize authentication, enabling organizations to enforce security policies such as multi-factor authentication (MFA), conditional access, and identity lifecycle management.

A Service Provider (SP), on the other hand, is an application or system that relies on an IdP to authenticate users. Instead of managing authentication independently, an SP delegates the process to a trusted IdP, which validates the user's identity and grants access accordingly. This approach simplifies access management, as SPs do not need to store or process user credentials directly. Examples of SPs include cloud-based applications like Salesforce, Microsoft 365, and AWS, which integrate with identity providers to allow users to log in using their corporate credentials.

The interaction between IdPs and SPs follows a structured authentication flow, typically based on industry-standard protocols such as Security Assertion Markup Language (SAML), OpenID Connect (OIDC), and OAuth 2.0. When a user attempts to access a service provider, they are redirected to the IdP for authentication. If the authentication is successful, the IdP issues a security token or assertion, which is then sent back to the SP to grant the user access. This process eliminates the need for users to maintain separate login credentials for each service, improving security and user experience.

One of the key benefits of using an IdP is centralized identity management. By consolidating authentication processes within a single entity, organizations can enforce consistent security policies across all integrated applications. This approach enhances security by enabling features such as single sign-on (SSO), where users authenticate once and gain access to multiple services without re-entering credentials. It also allows for better compliance and auditing, as all authentication events are logged in a centralized system, making it easier to detect anomalies and enforce access policies.

Service providers benefit from IdP integration by reducing the complexity of user management. Without an IdP, SPs would need to maintain their own user databases, implement authentication mechanisms, and manage password policies. This decentralized approach increases security risks, as each SP may have different security standards, leading to inconsistencies and vulnerabilities. By relying on an IdP, SPs offload authentication responsibilities to a trusted entity, ensuring a higher level of security and compliance with industry best practices.

In federated identity environments, trust relationships between IdPs and SPs are established through metadata exchange and cryptographic signatures. When an organization integrates an IdP with an SP, it configures the SP to trust authentication assertions issued by the IdP. This trust is maintained through digital certificates and encryption keys, ensuring that authentication requests and responses cannot be tampered with or intercepted. Properly configuring these trust relationships is essential to preventing security breaches, as weak configurations or expired certificates can lead to authentication failures or unauthorized access.

A common use case for IdPs and SPs is workforce identity management in enterprises. Employees often need access to multiple applications, including internal business systems, third-party SaaS applications, and cloud platforms. By using an IdP, organizations can provide seamless authentication while enforcing role-based access control (RBAC) to ensure users only have access to the services necessary for their job functions. Additionally, when employees leave the company, their access can be revoked centrally from the IdP, ensuring they no longer have access to any associated service providers.

Beyond workforce identity, IdPs and SPs also play a vital role in customer identity and access management (CIAM). Companies that offer online services, such as e-commerce platforms, streaming services, and financial applications, often integrate with social identity providers like Google, Facebook, and Apple. This integration allows customers to log in using their existing social media credentials instead of creating new accounts, simplifying the onboarding process and improving user experience. However, in these scenarios, businesses must carefully manage user data and ensure compliance with privacy regulations such as GDPR and CCPA.

Security is a major consideration in the interaction between IdPs and SPs. Because IdPs handle authentication for multiple services, they are attractive targets for attackers. If an IdP is compromised, an attacker could potentially gain access to all connected SPs, making it crucial to implement strong security measures. Organizations must adopt best practices such as enforcing MFA, monitoring authentication logs for suspicious activities, and ensuring that IdP-to-SP communication is encrypted and securely signed. Additionally, adopting risk-based

authentication strategies, which dynamically adjust authentication requirements based on factors like device reputation and geographic location, can help mitigate risks.

The role of IdPs and SPs continues to evolve as identity management technologies advance. With the rise of passwordless authentication, biometric verification, and decentralized identity models, the traditional authentication landscape is shifting. Organizations are increasingly adopting cloud-based identity solutions that leverage artificial intelligence and machine learning to detect fraud, automate access decisions, and enhance security. Meanwhile, the emergence of blockchain-based identity providers promises to give users greater control over their digital identities while reducing reliance on centralized authentication systems.

As organizations continue to embrace digital transformation, the relationship between Identity Providers and Service Providers remains a cornerstone of secure and efficient identity management. By leveraging IdPs for authentication and SPs for service delivery, businesses can streamline user access, enhance security, and improve the overall user experience. The success of federated identity frameworks depends on well-defined trust relationships, secure authentication protocols, and continuous monitoring to ensure that identity-based threats are mitigated effectively.

Identity Federation Models and Use Cases

Identity federation enables users to access multiple applications and services across different organizations using a single authentication process. This approach eliminates the need for separate credentials for each system, improving security, user experience, and administrative efficiency. Federated identity management relies on trust relationships between identity providers (IdPs) and service providers (SPs), allowing authentication assertions to be securely exchanged without requiring users to log in multiple times. Different models of identity federation exist, each designed to address specific business and security needs.

One of the most common identity federation models is the hub-and-spoke model, where a central identity provider acts as an authentication hub for multiple service providers. In this setup, the IdP is responsible for verifying user identities and issuing authentication assertions that SPs trust. This model is widely used in enterprises where employees need to access various business applications using a single set of credentials. By consolidating authentication within a central IdP, organizations can enforce consistent security policies, such as multi-factor authentication (MFA) and session expiration rules. Additionally, auditing and monitoring user activities become more manageable since all authentication events are logged in one place.

Another widely adopted model is the peer-to-peer federation model, where multiple organizations establish direct trust relationships without relying on a central IdP. In this model, each organization maintains its own identity provider, and authentication requests are exchanged directly between trusted partners. This approach is commonly used in business-to-business (B2B) scenarios where different companies collaborate and need to provide seamless access to shared resources. For example, a supplier may need to access an enterprise customer's procurement portal using their existing corporate credentials, eliminating the need to create and manage separate accounts.

A more decentralized approach is the circle of trust model, which involves multiple identity providers and service providers forming a federation where authentication assertions can be accepted across all participating entities. Unlike the hub-and-spoke model, where a single IdP is responsible for authentication, the circle of trust allows multiple IdPs to coexist while enforcing common security policies. This model is often used in government, healthcare, and academic institutions where multiple organizations need to authenticate users while maintaining their own identity management systems. The trust framework defines the security requirements and protocols that all members must adhere to, ensuring interoperability and compliance.

The bridge model extends identity federation across different authentication protocols, enabling interoperability between systems that use different standards. Organizations may use a mix of Security Assertion Markup Language (SAML), OAuth 2.0, and OpenID Connect

(OIDC) depending on their technology stack. A federation bridge acts as an intermediary that translates authentication assertions between different protocols, allowing users to access services regardless of the authentication mechanism used. This model is particularly useful for enterprises that undergo mergers and acquisitions, where different IAM systems need to be integrated without requiring users to switch authentication methods.

Identity federation is applied across various industries to streamline authentication and access management. One of the most prevalent use cases is enterprise single sign-on (SSO), where employees need seamless access to corporate applications, whether on-premises or in the cloud. Large organizations often integrate with cloud-based identity providers such as Microsoft Entra ID, Okta, or Ping Identity to provide federated authentication across multiple SaaS applications. By enabling SSO through identity federation, employees can log in once and access services like Salesforce, Microsoft 365, and AWS without having to re-enter credentials. This reduces password fatigue and minimizes security risks associated with credential reuse.

In the healthcare sector, identity federation plays a crucial role in enabling secure access to electronic health records (EHR) across different institutions. Doctors, nurses, and other healthcare providers often need to access patient data stored in systems maintained by various hospitals, insurance companies, and government agencies. By implementing a federated identity model, healthcare organizations can ensure that authorized personnel can securely access patient records without requiring multiple login credentials. This approach also supports compliance with regulatory frameworks such as HIPAA, which mandates strict controls over access to sensitive health information.

The higher education sector also benefits from identity federation through initiatives such as eduGAIN and InCommon, which enable students, faculty, and researchers to access academic resources across multiple institutions. Universities and research organizations use federated identity to allow students to log in to shared platforms, such as online learning portals, library systems, and collaborative research environments, using their home institution's credentials. This eliminates the need for separate accounts and simplifies access to educational resources while maintaining security and privacy.

A growing use case for identity federation is in the government and public sector, where citizens need to access various digital services provided by different agencies. Governments are increasingly adopting federated identity solutions to offer citizens a unified login experience for accessing services such as tax filings, social security, and healthcare benefits. By integrating national identity providers with government portals, users can authenticate once and securely access multiple services without creating separate accounts for each agency. This approach improves efficiency, reduces administrative overhead, and enhances the user experience for citizens.

Identity federation is also critical in the financial services industry, where banks, payment providers, and fintech companies need to authenticate customers while ensuring compliance with stringent security regulations. Federated authentication allows customers to access online banking, investment platforms, and third-party financial services using a single set of credentials, often secured with multi-factor authentication. Open Banking initiatives rely on federated identity frameworks such as OAuth 2.0 to facilitate secure data sharing between financial institutions and third-party service providers while maintaining user control over their financial information.

Another emerging use case for identity federation is in the retail and e-commerce sector, where businesses integrate with third-party authentication providers to streamline customer access to online shopping platforms. Many retailers allow customers to sign in using their Google, Apple, or Facebook accounts instead of creating separate credentials. This not only enhances convenience for customers but also reduces the risk of credential stuffing attacks, where attackers use leaked username-password combinations from data breaches to gain unauthorized access to accounts.

As organizations continue to adopt cloud computing, remote work, and digital transformation initiatives, identity federation is becoming a cornerstone of modern IAM strategies. The ability to establish trust relationships between identity providers and service providers simplifies authentication, enhances security, and improves user experience across multiple domains. By leveraging different federation models, organizations can create flexible and scalable authentication architectures that meet their business needs while ensuring compliance with security and privacy regulations.

Security Considerations in Identity Management

Identity management is a critical aspect of modern cybersecurity, ensuring that users and systems are authenticated, authorized, and monitored effectively. As organizations increasingly rely on cloud services, federated identity, and remote work environments, securing identity management systems has become more complex and essential. Cyber threats targeting user credentials, identity providers, and authentication mechanisms continue to evolve, requiring organizations to implement robust security measures to protect sensitive information and prevent unauthorized access.

One of the most significant security concerns in identity management is credential theft. Attackers frequently use phishing, social engineering, and credential stuffing attacks to gain access to user accounts. Phishing remains a primary attack vector, where malicious actors trick users into providing their login credentials through deceptive emails, fake login pages, or fraudulent messages. Credential stuffing involves using leaked username-password combinations from previous data breaches to attempt unauthorized access to multiple services. Since many users reuse passwords across different platforms, a single compromised credential can lead to a widespread security breach. Organizations must enforce strong password policies, implement multi-factor authentication (MFA), and educate users about recognizing phishing attempts to mitigate these risks.

Multi-factor authentication (MFA) is one of the most effective ways to enhance security in identity management. By requiring additional verification factors beyond a password, MFA significantly reduces the risk of unauthorized access, even if credentials are compromised. Common MFA methods include one-time passcodes sent via SMS or email, authentication apps, biometric authentication (such as fingerprint or facial recognition), and hardware security tokens. However, not all MFA methods are equally secure. SMS-based authentication, for example, is vulnerable to SIM swapping attacks, where attackers transfer a victim's phone number to a new SIM card and intercept authentication codes. Organizations should consider implementing more secure MFA options, such as app-based authenticators or hardware-based tokens like FIDO2 security keys.

Another major security consideration in identity management is privileged access management (PAM). Privileged accounts, such as system administrators, IT personnel, and executives with elevated access rights, are high-value targets for cybercriminals. If compromised, these accounts can provide attackers with unrestricted access to critical systems and sensitive data. Implementing least privilege access, where users receive only the minimum permissions required for their job functions, helps reduce the risk of privilege escalation attacks. Additionally, privileged access should be tightly controlled through just-in-time (JIT) access mechanisms, session monitoring, and automatic deactivation of inactive privileged accounts.

Identity federation and single sign-on (SSO) solutions introduce additional security considerations. While federated authentication simplifies access management by allowing users to authenticate once and access multiple services, it also centralizes authentication, making identity providers (IdPs) a prime target for attackers. If an IdP is compromised, an attacker could potentially access all connected service providers (SPs), leading to a significant security breach. To mitigate this risk, organizations must implement strong encryption for authentication tokens, enforce MFA at the IdP level, and regularly monitor authentication logs for suspicious activities.

Session management is another crucial factor in securing identity management. Once a user is authenticated, their session remains active until it expires or they log out. If session tokens are not properly secured, attackers can hijack active sessions and gain unauthorized access without needing to re-enter credentials. Implementing secure session management practices, such as automatic session expiration, token revocation, and binding tokens to specific devices or IP addresses, helps prevent session hijacking attacks. Additionally, organizations should use HTTP-only and secure cookies to protect session tokens from cross-site scripting (XSS) attacks.

The adoption of cloud-based identity and access management (IAM) solutions introduces challenges related to third-party security risks. Many organizations rely on cloud identity providers such as Microsoft Entra ID, Okta, and Google Workspace to manage authentication and access control. While these providers implement robust security measures, organizations must still configure their IAM settings correctly to prevent misconfigurations that could expose sensitive data. Common security misconfigurations include overly permissive access controls, misconfigured identity federation settings, and inadequate monitoring of access logs. Organizations should conduct regular security audits, enforce role-based access control (RBAC), and apply least privilege principles to minimize risks associated with cloud-based IAM solutions.

Compliance and regulatory requirements also play a critical role in identity management security. Many industries are subject to strict data protection laws and security frameworks, such as the General Data Protection Regulation (GDPR), the Health Insurance Portability and Accountability Act (HIPAA), and the Payment Card Industry Data Security Standard (PCI DSS). These regulations require organizations to implement strong identity security measures, including user authentication controls, access logging, and data encryption. Failure to comply with these regulations can result in significant legal and financial penalties. Organizations must ensure that their IAM systems align with relevant compliance requirements and conduct regular security assessments to maintain compliance.

Zero Trust security models are becoming increasingly relevant in identity management, shifting the traditional security mindset from trusting internal users by default to continuously verifying every access request. The Zero Trust approach assumes that no user or device should be inherently trusted, even if they are inside the corporate network. Identity-based security in a Zero Trust model involves continuous authentication, adaptive access policies, and risk-based authentication mechanisms. For example, if a user attempts to log in from an unfamiliar location or device, the system may prompt for additional verification or deny access altogether. This approach significantly reduces the risk of unauthorized access and insider threats.

Artificial intelligence (AI) and machine learning are also being integrated into identity management to enhance security. AI-driven identity security solutions analyze user behavior patterns to detect anomalies and identify potential threats. For example, if an employee suddenly attempts to access a system they have never used before or downloads an unusually large amount of data, AI-based monitoring tools can flag this behavior as suspicious and trigger security alerts or access restrictions. These intelligent security mechanisms provide organizations with real-time threat detection and response capabilities, strengthening overall identity security.

As cyber threats continue to evolve, organizations must adopt a proactive approach to securing identity management. Implementing strong authentication mechanisms, enforcing least privilege access, continuously monitoring user activity, and leveraging advanced security technologies are essential to protecting user identities and preventing unauthorized access. Identity security is not a one-time implementation but an ongoing process that requires continuous evaluation and adaptation to emerging threats. By prioritizing security considerations in identity management, organizations can safeguard their systems, protect sensitive data, and maintain trust in their digital infrastructure.

The Basics of SAML (Security Assertion Markup Language)

Security Assertion Markup Language (SAML) is a widely used standard for enabling secure, federated authentication and Single Sign-On (SSO) between identity providers (IdPs) and service providers (SPs).

Developed by the OASIS consortium, SAML provides a framework for exchanging authentication and authorization data in a standardized XML format. By leveraging SAML, organizations can allow users to authenticate once with an identity provider and gain seamless access to multiple applications without needing to log in separately to each one. This approach improves security, reduces password fatigue, and enhances user experience.

At its core, SAML enables identity federation by establishing a trust relationship between an IdP, which verifies user identities, and an SP, which provides access to applications or services. When a user attempts to access an SP, the SP delegates authentication to the IdP, which then issues a SAML assertion containing the user's authentication details. The SP processes this assertion, verifies its authenticity, and grants access accordingly. This method eliminates the need for service providers to store and manage user credentials, reducing security risks associated with password management.

A SAML-based authentication flow typically follows a structured sequence of interactions between the user, the IdP, and the SP. The process begins when a user attempts to access a protected resource on an SP. If the user is not already authenticated, the SP redirects them to the IdP for authentication. The IdP prompts the user for credentials and verifies their identity. Upon successful authentication, the IdP generates a SAML assertion, which contains details about the authenticated user, including their identity attributes, roles, and permissions. This assertion is then digitally signed and sent back to the SP. The SP validates the assertion, extracts the relevant user information, and grants access to the requested resource.

A key component of SAML is the SAML assertion, which serves as the mechanism for transmitting authentication and authorization data between the IdP and SP. SAML assertions are structured XML documents containing three primary components: authentication statements, attribute statements, and authorization decision statements. The authentication statement confirms that a user has successfully authenticated with the IdP at a specific time using a particular method, such as a password, multi-factor authentication, or biometric verification. Attribute statements provide additional user information, such as email addresses, department names, or access levels. Authorization decision statements specify whether the user is permitted to access certain resources based on predefined policies.

SAML operates using two primary communication bindings: HTTP Redirect Binding and HTTP POST Binding. The HTTP Redirect Binding method is commonly used when a user initiates authentication from an SP and is redirected to the IdP. This method is efficient for handling authentication requests but has size limitations for the transmitted messages. The HTTP POST Binding method, on the other hand, transmits authentication responses securely via an HTML form post, ensuring that larger SAML assertions can be processed without truncation. Both methods rely on secure transport mechanisms, such as HTTPS, to protect authentication data from interception.

One of the main advantages of SAML is its support for Single Sign-On (SSO), which allows users to authenticate once and gain access to multiple SPs without repeated login prompts. This feature is particularly useful in enterprise environments where employees need to access a range of business applications, including email services, collaboration tools, and customer relationship management (CRM) platforms. By using SAML-based SSO, organizations can enhance productivity, reduce administrative overhead, and minimize security risks associated with password reuse.

Security considerations are an essential aspect of SAML implementations. Because SAML assertions contain sensitive authentication and authorization data, they must be protected against tampering and replay attacks. Digital signatures ensure that assertions are issued by a trusted IdP and have not been altered in transit. Encryption mechanisms further enhance security by protecting the confidentiality of assertion contents. Organizations must also implement strict token expiration policies to prevent unauthorized reuse of authentication assertions. Regular audits and monitoring of SAML authentication logs can help detect and mitigate potential security threats.

SAML is widely adopted in various industries and use cases. In cloud computing, many software-as-a-service (SaaS) providers, such as Salesforce, Google Workspace, and Microsoft 365, support SAML-based authentication to integrate with enterprise identity management systems. In higher education, SAML enables federated access to academic resources, allowing students and faculty members to use their institutional credentials to log in to research databases, online learning platforms, and library services. Government agencies also leverage SAML to facilitate secure identity federation across departments and service portals, ensuring seamless authentication while maintaining strict security and compliance requirements.

Despite its benefits, SAML also has some limitations. As an XML-based protocol, SAML messages can be relatively large and complex compared to modern authentication standards such as OAuth 2.0 and OpenID Connect, which use lightweight JSON Web Tokens (JWTs). Additionally, implementing SAML can be challenging due to its reliance on XML parsing, digital certificates, and complex configurations. Organizations must ensure that both the IdP and SP are correctly configured to support SAML authentication flows, including metadata exchange, signature validation, and assertion decryption.

SAML remains a foundational technology in federated identity management, providing a reliable and standardized way to enable secure authentication and Single Sign-On across disparate systems. While newer authentication protocols such as OAuth 2.0 and OpenID Connect offer alternative approaches for modern applications, SAML continues to be a preferred choice for enterprise and government environments where security, interoperability, and trust are paramount. Organizations implementing SAML should carefully consider security best practices, ensure proper configuration of IdP and SP integrations, and continuously monitor authentication events to maintain a secure and efficient identity management framework.

OAuth 2.0: Delegated Authorization for Applications

OAuth 2.0 is a widely adopted framework that enables secure, delegated authorization for applications without exposing user credentials. Designed as an improvement over its predecessor, OAuth 1.0, it provides a more flexible and scalable approach to granting third-party applications limited access to user resources. Unlike traditional authentication methods, which require users to share their passwords with multiple services, OAuth 2.0 allows users to grant applications specific permissions using access tokens. This approach enhances security, improves user experience, and minimizes the risks associated with password sharing.

At its core, OAuth 2.0 separates authentication from authorization. Authentication verifies the identity of a user, while authorization determines what actions an application can perform on behalf of that user. OAuth 2.0 enables users to authenticate with a trusted identity provider and grant applications permission to access their resources without revealing their login credentials. This delegation mechanism is commonly used in scenarios where third-party services need controlled access to user data, such as when a mobile app requests permission to access a user's contacts, calendar, or cloud storage.

OAuth 2.0 operates through a structured authorization flow involving four primary roles: the resource owner, the client application, the authorization server, and the resource server. The resource owner is the user who owns the protected data. The client application is the service requesting access to the user's data. The authorization server is responsible for authenticating the user and issuing access tokens, while the resource server hosts the protected resources and verifies access tokens before granting requests. These roles work together to enable secure and efficient authorization.

The authorization process begins when a client application requests permission to access user resources. The user is redirected to the authorization server, where they authenticate and review the requested permissions. If the user approves the request, the authorization server issues an authorization grant, which the client application exchanges for an access token. This access token is then used to make authorized requests to the resource server. Access tokens are typically short-lived and can be refreshed using refresh tokens, which extend access without requiring the user to reauthenticate.

OAuth 2.0 defines multiple authorization grant types to accommodate different application scenarios. The authorization code grant is the most secure and commonly used flow, especially for web applications and native mobile apps. In this flow, the client application first receives an authorization code from the authorization server, which it exchanges for an access token. This process prevents direct exposure of access tokens to the client, reducing the risk of token interception.

The implicit grant was originally designed for browser-based applications but is now discouraged due to security vulnerabilities. In this flow, the authorization server directly issues an access token without an intermediate authorization code. However, since access tokens are exposed in the browser's URL, they are susceptible to theft through malicious scripts or man-in-the-middle attacks.

The client credentials grant is used when a client application needs to access its own resources rather than acting on behalf of a user. This flow is commonly used in machine-to-machine communications, where an application, such as a microservice, requires authentication to interact with another system. Since no user is involved, the client application authenticates itself using a client ID and secret, and the authorization server issues an access token accordingly.

The resource owner password credentials grant allows users to provide their username and password directly to the client application, which then exchanges them for an access token. This flow is considered less secure than others because it requires users to share their credentials with the client application, violating OAuth's principle of not exposing passwords. It is generally only recommended for trusted applications under strict security controls.

The device authorization grant is designed for devices with limited input capabilities, such as smart TVs and IoT devices. In this flow, the user is provided with a code to enter on a separate device, such as a smartphone or computer, to authorize access. This approach eliminates the need to enter credentials directly on the limited-input device, improving security and usability.

Security is a crucial aspect of OAuth 2.0 implementations. One of the main security challenges is access token leakage, where an attacker obtains a valid access token and uses it to gain unauthorized access. To mitigate this risk, tokens should be transmitted securely over HTTPS, stored securely on client devices, and have short expiration times.

Another security concern is token replay attacks, where a stolen token is reused by an attacker. OAuth 2.0 mitigates this risk by using refresh tokens, which are securely stored and used to obtain new access tokens without requiring the user to reauthenticate. Refresh tokens should be stored securely, and their usage should be monitored to detect anomalies.

OAuth 2.0 also supports scope-based access control, which allows users to grant applications specific permissions rather than full access to their data. Scopes define the level of access an application is requesting, such as read-only access to emails or the ability to post on behalf of a user. By limiting the permissions granted to applications, OAuth reduces the risk of unauthorized actions.

OAuth 2.0 is widely used in modern identity and access management. Many large technology companies, including Google, Facebook, Microsoft, and GitHub, use OAuth 2.0 to enable third-party applications to integrate with their platforms securely. For example, when a user logs into a website using their Google account, OAuth 2.0 facilitates the authentication and authorization process, ensuring that the website never sees the user's actual Google credentials.

Another common use case for OAuth 2.0 is API security. Many cloud services and enterprise systems use OAuth to authenticate API requests and restrict access based on user roles and permissions. This approach is particularly useful in microservices architectures, where multiple services need to interact securely while maintaining fine-grained access controls.

OAuth 2.0 also plays a crucial role in mobile application security. Mobile apps frequently use OAuth to authenticate users with external identity providers while ensuring that sensitive credentials are never stored on the device. This reduces the risk of credential theft due to device compromise or malware.

As identity and security needs evolve, OAuth 2.0 continues to be a cornerstone of secure, delegated authorization. While it addresses many security concerns, proper implementation is essential to prevent vulnerabilities. Developers and organizations must follow best practices such as using the authorization code grant with PKCE (Proof Key for Code Exchange) for mobile and browser-based applications, enforcing token expiration policies, and continuously monitoring token usage to detect suspicious activity. By leveraging OAuth 2.0 effectively, organizations can provide secure and seamless access to user resources while minimizing security risks.

OpenID Connect: Authentication on Top of OAuth 2.0

OpenID Connect (OIDC) is an authentication protocol built on top of OAuth 2.0 that enables secure user authentication and identity verification for web, mobile, and API-based applications. While OAuth 2.0 is primarily designed for authorization—allowing applications to access resources on behalf of a user—it does not provide a standardized way to authenticate users or retrieve identity information. OpenID Connect fills this gap by extending OAuth 2.0 with authentication capabilities, allowing applications to verify users' identities while also enabling Single Sign-On (SSO) across multiple platforms.

At its core, OpenID Connect introduces the concept of an ID token, a JSON Web Token (JWT) that contains identity-related claims about the authenticated user. Unlike OAuth 2.0 access tokens, which grant permissions to access user resources, ID tokens are specifically designed to convey authentication information. These tokens include details such as the user's unique identifier (subject), the issuing identity provider (IdP), authentication timestamp, and optional profile attributes such as name, email, and roles. Because ID tokens are digitally signed, they can be securely verified by applications without direct interaction with the identity provider.

OpenID Connect operates through an authentication flow similar to OAuth 2.0 but with additional steps to support identity verification. When a user attempts to log in to an application, they are redirected to the OpenID Provider (OP), which acts as the identity provider. The user authenticates with the OP using their credentials, biometric authentication, or other methods. Upon successful authentication, the OP issues an ID token, along with an optional access token, and sends them back to the client application. The client verifies the ID token's signature and extracts identity claims to establish the user's session.

One of the key benefits of OpenID Connect is its support for federated identity and Single Sign-On (SSO). By allowing users to authenticate once with an OpenID provider and access multiple applications without re-entering credentials, OIDC simplifies the login experience while improving security. This approach is widely used in enterprise environments where employees need seamless access to multiple business applications using corporate credentials. Similarly, consumer-facing services, such as Google, Microsoft, and Apple, use OpenID Connect to enable users to log in to third-party websites and applications without creating separate accounts.

OpenID Connect defines several authentication flows, also known as grant types, to accommodate different application scenarios. The authorization code flow is the most secure and commonly used method, particularly for web and mobile applications. In this flow, the client application first receives an authorization code from the OpenID provider and then exchanges it for an ID token and access token. This process prevents direct exposure of sensitive tokens in the browser, reducing the risk of token theft.

The implicit flow was originally designed for single-page applications (SPAs) and JavaScript-based clients, allowing them to receive ID tokens directly from the OpenID provider without a backend server. However, due to security concerns, such as token interception and lack of refresh token support, the implicit flow is no longer recommended for new implementations. Instead, modern SPAs use the authorization code flow with Proof Key for Code Exchange (PKCE), which mitigates code interception attacks by requiring an additional verification step when exchanging the authorization code for tokens.

The hybrid flow is a combination of the authorization code and implicit flows, providing flexibility for applications that need both immediate access to an ID token and the ability to retrieve an access token securely from a backend server. This flow is commonly used in scenarios where applications need to display user identity information immediately while also making API requests with additional security measures.

Security is a crucial aspect of OpenID Connect implementations. Because ID tokens contain authentication claims, they must be validated properly to prevent identity spoofing. Applications receiving ID tokens must verify their digital signatures using the public keys provided by the OpenID provider. Additionally, tokens should be checked for expiration timestamps and audience (aud) claims to ensure they were issued for the intended application.

To further enhance security, OpenID Connect supports token revocation and session management mechanisms. If a user logs out or revokes access to an application, the identity provider can invalidate tokens and notify relying applications to terminate active sessions. This prevents unauthorized access in case a user's device is lost or compromised. Organizations implementing OpenID Connect should also enforce secure token storage practices, using encrypted storage mechanisms to protect ID tokens from theft.

A major advantage of OpenID Connect is its seamless integration with OAuth 2.0 APIs. Because OIDC extends OAuth 2.0, applications using OpenID Connect can also request access tokens to interact with external APIs on behalf of authenticated users. This is particularly useful in scenarios such as cloud-based identity services, where applications need both authentication (via ID tokens) and authorization (via access tokens) to access user data stored in cloud platforms.

OpenID Connect is widely used in social login implementations, allowing users to authenticate with their Google, Facebook, or Apple accounts instead of creating new credentials for every website they visit. This approach reduces password fatigue, improves user experience, and minimizes security risks associated with weak or reused passwords. Businesses integrating social login can streamline user onboarding while ensuring strong identity verification through established OpenID providers.

In enterprise environments, OpenID Connect plays a crucial role in securing workforce authentication. Many organizations use OpenID Connect to enable SSO for business applications, integrating with identity providers such as Microsoft Entra ID, Okta, and Ping Identity. This allows employees to access corporate applications securely without managing multiple passwords, reducing administrative overhead and improving compliance with security policies.

The adoption of passwordless authentication is also growing with OpenID Connect. Identity providers can support passwordless login methods, such as biometric authentication, hardware security keys (FIDO2/WebAuthn), and mobile push authentication, using OpenID Connect as the authentication framework. This eliminates the reliance on passwords, reducing phishing risks and improving security posture.

As digital identity management evolves, OpenID Connect continues to be a foundational authentication protocol, providing a standardized, interoperable, and secure way to verify user identities across diverse applications. Its integration with OAuth 2.0 allows organizations to build scalable authentication and authorization systems, supporting modern security best practices while enhancing the user experience. Whether for enterprise SSO, social login, or API security, OpenID Connect remains a crucial component of modern identity architectures.

JWTs (JSON Web Tokens) and Their Role in SSO

JSON Web Tokens (JWTs) have become a fundamental component in modern authentication and authorization frameworks, particularly in Single Sign-On (SSO) implementations. JWTs provide a lightweight, secure, and efficient way to transmit authentication and identity information between different parties, making them an essential tool for federated identity systems. By enabling secure token-based authentication, JWTs help streamline user access across multiple applications and services without requiring repeated logins. Their widespread adoption in web and mobile applications, APIs, and cloud-based services highlights their significance in identity management.

A JWT is a compact, URL-safe token format that encodes authentication claims in a JSON structure. These tokens are self-contained, meaning they carry all the necessary information required for authentication without relying on a centralized session store. This makes JWTs particularly useful for stateless authentication mechanisms, where servers do not need to maintain session data for each user. Instead, the token itself contains all relevant details and can be validated independently by any system that trusts the issuing authority.

A standard JWT consists of three parts: the header, the payload, and the signature. The header defines the type of token (JWT) and the algorithm used for signing, such as HMAC SHA-256 or RSA. The payload contains claims, which are key-value pairs representing identity-related information, such as the user ID, email address, and expiration time. The signature is generated by encoding the header and payload with a secret key or private key, ensuring the integrity and authenticity of the token. This structure makes JWTs tamper-resistant, as any modification to the token will invalidate the signature.

JWTs play a crucial role in enabling Single Sign-On (SSO), a mechanism that allows users to authenticate once and gain access to multiple applications without needing to re-enter credentials. In an SSO environment, an identity provider (IdP) authenticates the user and issues a JWT that is then passed to various service providers (SPs).

Each SP can validate the JWT independently without needing to contact the IdP, significantly reducing authentication latency and improving system scalability.

In a typical SSO workflow using JWTs, a user logs into an identity provider, which verifies their credentials and generates a signed JWT containing authentication claims. This token is then presented to different service providers, which validate its signature, extract user information, and grant access accordingly. Since JWTs are self-contained, they eliminate the need for SPs to maintain session states, making them an ideal solution for distributed applications and microservices architectures.

One of the key advantages of JWTs in SSO is their support for federated identity systems. Federated identity allows users to authenticate with a single identity provider and access multiple third-party applications seamlessly. JWTs facilitate this process by serving as a standardized authentication mechanism that different applications can trust. This is particularly useful in enterprise environments where employees need access to cloud-based services such as Google Workspace, Microsoft 365, and Salesforce using their corporate credentials.

Security is a critical aspect of JWT usage in SSO implementations. Because JWTs are often used to grant access to protected resources, they must be properly secured to prevent unauthorized access. One common security risk is token theft, where an attacker gains access to a valid JWT and uses it to impersonate a user. To mitigate this risk, organizations should enforce token expiration policies, requiring users to refresh their tokens periodically. Additionally, storing JWTs securely—such as in HTTP-only cookies instead of local storage—helps protect them from cross-site scripting (XSS) attacks.

Another security consideration is token validation. Since JWTs are signed but not encrypted by default, their contents can be decoded by anyone who has access to the token. While this does not compromise security if sensitive data is not included in the payload, organizations should use encryption for JWTs that contain confidential information. Additionally, service providers must verify the token's signature using the public key of the issuing identity provider to ensure its authenticity and integrity.

The role of JWTs in API authentication is another important use case. Many modern applications rely on APIs to handle user authentication and authorization, particularly in cloud-based and microservices environments. In these scenarios, JWTs serve as bearer tokens that clients present when making API requests. The API server validates the token, extracts user claims, and determines access rights based on the encoded information. This approach eliminates the need for session-based authentication, making JWTs an ideal solution for stateless and scalable API architectures.

OAuth 2.0 and OpenID Connect (OIDC) both leverage JWTs to enhance authentication and authorization workflows. In an OAuth 2.0 implementation, JWTs are often used as access tokens that grant clients permission to access protected resources on behalf of a user. Similarly, OpenID Connect extends OAuth 2.0 by introducing ID tokens, which are JWTs specifically designed to carry authentication claims. These ID tokens enable applications to verify user identities without directly interacting with the identity provider, facilitating seamless authentication experiences.

Beyond authentication, JWTs also support role-based access control (RBAC) by embedding user roles and permissions within the token payload. When a service provider receives a JWT, it can inspect the included claims to determine the user's authorization level. For example, an enterprise application might use JWTs to enforce different levels of access for employees based on their department or job role. By incorporating authorization data directly into tokens, organizations can implement fine-grained access controls without relying on additional database lookups.

Despite their advantages, JWTs are not suitable for all authentication scenarios. Because JWTs are self-contained and do not require a centralized session store, revoking a compromised token before its expiration can be challenging. Unlike traditional session-based authentication, where sessions can be invalidated instantly, JWTs remain valid until they expire. To address this limitation, organizations can implement token revocation mechanisms, such as maintaining a blacklist of revoked tokens or using short-lived JWTs with frequent refresh tokens.

The growing adoption of JWTs in authentication and authorization systems highlights their importance in modern identity management. By enabling secure, efficient, and scalable authentication workflows, JWTs facilitate seamless Single Sign-On experiences, enhance API security, and support federated identity frameworks. However, proper implementation is crucial to ensuring their security and effectiveness. Organizations must follow best practices, including enforcing token expiration, securing token storage, and validating signatures, to maximize the benefits of JWTs in identity and access management.

Kerberos Authentication and Single Sign-On

Kerberos is a network authentication protocol designed to provide secure authentication over untrusted networks. Developed at the Massachusetts Institute of Technology (MIT) in the 1980s, Kerberos has become a foundational component of enterprise security, particularly in environments that require Single Sign-On (SSO). By using strong cryptographic techniques and a trusted third-party authentication system, Kerberos enables secure identity verification while protecting against common security threats, such as password interception and replay attacks. It is widely used in Microsoft Active Directory, Unix-based systems, and enterprise authentication frameworks.

At its core, Kerberos relies on a centralized authentication service known as the Key Distribution Center (KDC). The KDC is responsible for issuing time-sensitive authentication tokens called tickets, which allow users and services to authenticate securely without transmitting plaintext passwords. The KDC consists of two main components: the Authentication Server (AS), which verifies user credentials and issues initial tickets, and the Ticket Granting Server (TGS), which provides service-specific tickets that allow users to access network resources. These tickets are encrypted and time-bound, ensuring secure communication while reducing the risk of credential theft.

A typical Kerberos authentication process begins when a user attempts to log in to a Kerberos-enabled system. The user provides their credentials, which are used to request an initial ticket, known as a Ticket Granting Ticket (TGT), from the Authentication Server. The AS verifies the credentials and issues the TGT, which is encrypted with a secret key known only to the KDC. The TGT serves as proof that the user has successfully authenticated and can now request access to additional services without re-entering their credentials.

Once the TGT is obtained, the user can request access to specific network resources. To do this, the client presents the TGT to the Ticket Granting Server, which verifies the ticket's validity and issues a Service Ticket for the requested resource. This service ticket is then presented to the target service, which validates the ticket and grants access. Because the service ticket is encrypted and timestamped, it ensures that authentication requests are legitimate and have not been tampered with. This process allows users to authenticate once and access multiple services seamlessly, making Kerberos an effective SSO solution.

One of the key advantages of Kerberos-based authentication is its resistance to password-based attacks. Since user passwords are never transmitted over the network in plaintext, attackers cannot intercept them using packet-sniffing techniques. Instead, Kerberos relies on symmetric encryption, where authentication requests and responses are secured using secret keys shared between the KDC, clients, and services. This design significantly reduces the risk of credential theft and mitigates common threats such as replay attacks, where an attacker captures and reuses authentication data to gain unauthorized access.

Kerberos also supports mutual authentication, ensuring that both the client and the server verify each other's identities before communication begins. This prevents man-in-the-middle (MITM) attacks, where an attacker impersonates a legitimate service to steal credentials or intercept sensitive data. Mutual authentication is particularly important in enterprise environments where users access critical resources, such as file servers, databases, and enterprise applications. By verifying both parties, Kerberos establishes a trusted communication channel that enhances security.

Microsoft Active Directory (AD) is one of the most prominent implementations of Kerberos, using it as the default authentication protocol for domain-joined computers. In an Active Directory environment, Kerberos enables users to log in once and gain access to network resources, including file shares, email services, and enterprise applications, without needing to re-enter their credentials. This integration allows organizations to implement robust security policies, enforce role-based access control (RBAC), and centrally manage user authentication across the enterprise.

Kerberos authentication is also widely used in Unix and Linux environments, where it integrates with services such as SSH, NFS, and LDAP. In these systems, Kerberos provides seamless authentication while maintaining strong security controls. Many large organizations use Kerberos to authenticate users accessing Unix-based servers, ensuring that only authorized personnel can log in and execute privileged commands. The protocol's ability to work across different operating systems makes it a valuable tool for securing heterogeneous IT environments.

Despite its advantages, Kerberos authentication has some challenges and limitations. One of the main challenges is time synchronization. Because Kerberos relies on time-stamped tickets to prevent replay attacks, all participating systems must be synchronized with the same time source, typically using the Network Time Protocol (NTP). If there is significant time drift between the client, KDC, or service provider, authentication requests may fail due to expired or invalid tickets. Organizations must ensure that time synchronization is properly configured to avoid authentication failures.

Another challenge is the single point of failure associated with the Key Distribution Center. If the KDC becomes unavailable, users will not be able to obtain new tickets, effectively preventing authentication and access to services. To mitigate this risk, enterprises typically deploy redundant KDC servers and implement failover mechanisms to ensure high availability. Load balancing and clustering strategies are also used to distribute authentication requests across multiple KDCs, reducing the risk of service disruptions.

Kerberos also requires strong security configurations to prevent potential attack vectors. For example, ticket lifetime policies must be carefully managed to balance security and usability. If tickets have excessively long lifetimes, they could be exploited by attackers who gain access to an active session. Conversely, if ticket lifetimes are too short, users may experience frequent authentication prompts, reducing the effectiveness of SSO. Organizations must define appropriate expiration policies based on their security requirements and user needs.

Additionally, service principal names (SPNs) must be properly configured to prevent security vulnerabilities. An SPN is a unique identifier for a service that Kerberos uses to issue tickets. If an attacker registers an unauthorized SPN, they could trick clients into sending authentication requests to a malicious service, potentially exposing credentials. To mitigate this risk, administrators should enforce strict controls over SPN registration and regularly audit their Active Directory environments for anomalies.

Kerberos continues to be a cornerstone of secure authentication in enterprise environments, providing a robust and scalable solution for Single Sign-On. Its strong encryption, mutual authentication, and centralized ticketing system make it a preferred choice for securing access to corporate networks, cloud-based services, and enterprise applications. While newer authentication protocols such as OAuth 2.0 and OpenID Connect have gained popularity for web and mobile applications, Kerberos remains a trusted and widely used authentication mechanism, particularly in on-premises IT infrastructures.

As organizations evolve their authentication strategies, Kerberos can be combined with modern security frameworks to enhance identity protection. For example, integrating Kerberos with multi-factor authentication (MFA) adds an extra layer of security by requiring users to verify their identities using biometric authentication, smart cards, or one-time passcodes. Similarly, Kerberos-based authentication can be extended to cloud environments using hybrid identity models, enabling seamless authentication across on-premises and cloud-based applications.

By implementing best practices, maintaining proper security configurations, and addressing potential challenges, organizations can effectively leverage Kerberos to provide strong authentication and Single Sign-On, ensuring secure and efficient access to enterprise resources.

LDAP and Active Directory in Identity Management

Lightweight Directory Access Protocol (LDAP) and Microsoft Active Directory (AD) are two essential components of identity and access management (IAM) in enterprise environments. These technologies enable organizations to manage user identities, enforce authentication policies, and control access to IT resources efficiently. LDAP serves as a protocol for querying and modifying directory services, while Active Directory is a directory service that integrates LDAP with additional security and authentication features. Together, they form the backbone of identity management in many corporate networks, providing centralized control over user accounts, devices, and access permissions.

LDAP was developed as a lightweight alternative to the older X.500 directory access protocol, designed to enable efficient access to directory information over a network. It follows a client-server model, where LDAP clients send requests to an LDAP server, which processes the queries and returns the requested directory information. The LDAP directory stores hierarchical data in a tree structure, known as the Directory Information Tree (DIT), where entries represent users, groups, computers, and other resources. Each entry in the directory is identified by a Distinguished Name (DN) and consists of attributes such as usernames, email addresses, passwords, and access permissions.

One of the primary use cases of LDAP in identity management is user authentication. When a user attempts to log in to a system or application, the authentication process typically involves querying the LDAP directory to verify the user's credentials. The client application sends a request containing the username and password, and the LDAP server checks the stored credentials to confirm the user's identity. If the credentials match, the user is granted access; otherwise, authentication is denied. LDAP supports multiple authentication mechanisms, including simple authentication with username and password, SASL (Simple Authentication and Security Layer), and binding with security certificates for stronger authentication.

In enterprise environments, LDAP is commonly used in Single Sign-On (SSO) solutions, allowing users to authenticate once and gain access to multiple services without re-entering their credentials. By centralizing user authentication, LDAP reduces password fatigue, enhances security, and simplifies user management. Many organizations integrate LDAP with other authentication protocols such as Kerberos, SAML, and OAuth 2.0 to enable seamless access across different platforms and applications.

Microsoft Active Directory (AD) builds upon LDAP by adding additional features tailored for enterprise identity management. Introduced with Windows 2000, Active Directory provides a comprehensive framework for managing user identities, security policies, and network resources in Windows-based environments. While AD uses LDAP as its underlying protocol for directory access, it also integrates Kerberos authentication, Group Policy management, and domain-based security controls to enhance IAM capabilities.

Active Directory organizes resources into a hierarchical structure known as the Active Directory Domain Services (AD DS). Within AD DS, organizations define domains, which serve as administrative boundaries for user accounts, computers, and security policies. Multiple domains can be grouped into forests, allowing organizations to manage different business units or geographical locations under a single identity infrastructure. Within each domain, objects such as users, groups, organizational units (OUs), and computers are organized in a structured manner, enabling administrators to apply granular security policies and access controls.

One of the key advantages of Active Directory is its centralized user management. Administrators can create and manage user accounts, assign roles, and enforce security policies from a single console, known as the Active Directory Users and Computers (ADUC) tool. This centralized approach reduces administrative overhead and ensures consistency across the organization. Additionally, AD supports Group Policy Objects (GPOs), which allow administrators to define security settings, software installations, and access controls across multiple devices.

Active Directory also plays a crucial role in network authentication. Windows-based networks rely on AD-integrated Kerberos authentication to provide secure login experiences for users. When a user logs into a Windows domain, their credentials are authenticated against the Active Directory database, and they receive a Kerberos ticket that grants access to authorized resources. This process eliminates the need for repeated authentication prompts, making AD a core component of enterprise SSO solutions.

Another important feature of Active Directory is its support for role-based access control (RBAC). By grouping users into security groups, administrators can assign permissions based on job functions rather than individual accounts. For example, all employees in the HR department can be added to an "HR Group," which grants them access to HR-related applications and file shares. This approach simplifies access management, reduces the risk of excessive permissions, and improves overall security.

LDAP and Active Directory are also widely used in federated identity management, enabling organizations to integrate their on-premises identity systems with cloud-based services. Many cloud platforms, such as Microsoft Entra ID (formerly Azure AD), Okta, and Google Workspace, provide LDAP connectors that allow seamless authentication using on-premises AD credentials. This integration enables organizations to extend their IAM capabilities beyond traditional network boundaries while maintaining centralized control over user identities.

Security is a critical aspect of LDAP and Active Directory implementations. Since these directory services store sensitive identity information, they must be properly secured against cyber threats. One of the most common attack vectors is LDAP enumeration, where attackers attempt to query an LDAP directory to gather information about users, groups, and systems. To prevent unauthorized access, organizations should implement LDAP access controls, enforce strong authentication mechanisms, and disable anonymous LDAP binds.

Another significant security concern is Active Directory privilege escalation, where attackers exploit misconfigurations or weak permissions to gain elevated privileges. To mitigate this risk, organizations should follow best practices such as limiting administrator privileges, regularly auditing AD configurations, and implementing Privileged Access Management (PAM) solutions. Additionally, monitoring and logging LDAP and AD authentication events can help detect suspicious activities, such as brute-force login attempts or unauthorized access requests.

As organizations increasingly adopt hybrid identity models, integrating on-premises AD with cloud-based identity providers has become a common practice. Microsoft Entra ID, for example, enables organizations to synchronize their AD users with cloud services, allowing employees to authenticate using the same credentials across both on-premises and cloud environments. This hybrid approach provides flexibility while ensuring strong identity governance and security controls.

LDAP and Active Directory continue to be fundamental components of modern identity management, providing organizations with scalable, secure, and centralized authentication frameworks. Whether used for on-premises authentication, cloud integration, or federated identity management, these technologies help businesses enforce security policies, streamline user access, and enhance IAM strategies across diverse IT environments. By implementing proper security configurations, integrating with modern authentication protocols, and adopting best practices, organizations can maximize the benefits of LDAP and Active Directory while mitigating security risks.

Passwordless Authentication: The Future of SSO

Passwordless authentication is transforming the way users access digital services, offering a more secure and convenient alternative to traditional password-based authentication. As organizations increasingly adopt Single Sign-On (SSO) solutions to simplify identity management, passwordless authentication is emerging as the next evolutionary step in securing user access. By eliminating the need for passwords, this approach reduces the risks associated with credential theft, phishing attacks, and password fatigue, while improving the overall user experience.

The reliance on passwords has long been a security challenge for organizations. Users often create weak passwords, reuse them across multiple accounts, or fall victim to phishing scams that trick them into revealing their credentials. Cybercriminals exploit these vulnerabilities through brute-force attacks, credential stuffing, and social engineering tactics, leading to widespread data breaches. Passwordless authentication addresses these issues by replacing passwords with more secure authentication methods, such as biometrics, security keys, and cryptographic authentication.

One of the most common forms of passwordless authentication is biometric authentication, which uses unique physical or behavioral characteristics to verify a user's identity. Fingerprint scanning, facial recognition, and voice authentication are widely used in smartphones, laptops, and enterprise authentication systems. These methods provide a seamless and secure login experience, as biometric data is unique to each user and cannot be easily guessed or stolen like a traditional password. Biometric authentication is also resistant to phishing attacks, as it does not rely on shared secrets that can be intercepted or manipulated.

Another popular approach to passwordless authentication is the use of hardware security keys. These small physical devices, such as YubiKeys or Google Titan Security Keys, generate cryptographic authentication tokens that verify a user's identity. When logging into a system, the user inserts the security key into a USB port or taps it on an NFC-enabled device to complete the authentication process. Since security keys use public-key cryptography, they eliminate the need for shared secrets, making them highly resistant to phishing, keylogging, and man-in-the-middle attacks.

One-time passcodes (OTPs) and push notifications are also widely used in passwordless authentication. OTPs are temporary codes generated by an authentication app, such as Microsoft Authenticator or Google Authenticator, and expire after a short period. Push notifications, on the other hand, send authentication requests directly to a user's mobile device, allowing them to approve or deny access with a single tap. While these methods enhance security by requiring possession of a trusted device, they are still susceptible to attacks such as SIM swapping and phishing if not properly implemented.

FIDO2, a standard developed by the Fast Identity Online (FIDO) Alliance and the World Wide Web Consortium (W3C), is at the forefront of passwordless authentication. FIDO2 enables strong, phishing-resistant authentication using public-key cryptography and biometric authentication. The WebAuthn (Web Authentication) component of FIDO2 allows users to authenticate to web applications using built-in biometric sensors or external security keys, eliminating the need for passwords. By integrating FIDO2 with SSO solutions, organizations can provide a seamless authentication experience while maintaining strong security controls.

In the context of Single Sign-On (SSO), passwordless authentication enhances both security and usability. SSO allows users to authenticate once and gain access to multiple applications without needing to re-enter their credentials. When combined with passwordless authentication, SSO eliminates the need for users to create and remember passwords entirely. This reduces the risk of credential theft and improves operational efficiency by minimizing helpdesk requests for password resets.

Enterprise environments are rapidly adopting passwordless authentication to improve security and compliance. Microsoft Entra ID (formerly Azure AD), Okta, and Ping Identity offer passwordless SSO solutions that integrate with enterprise applications, enabling users to authenticate using biometrics, security keys, or mobile authentication apps. By implementing passwordless authentication at the identity provider level, organizations can enforce strong authentication policies across all connected service providers while simplifying user access.

Passwordless authentication also enhances security in remote work and cloud environments. With employees accessing corporate resources from various devices and locations, traditional password-based authentication poses significant security risks. Cybercriminals target remote workers through phishing attacks, credential stuffing, and account takeovers. By adopting passwordless authentication, organizations can mitigate these risks by ensuring that only authorized users with secure authentication methods can access corporate systems.

While passwordless authentication offers numerous advantages, its implementation requires careful planning and consideration. Organizations must ensure that authentication methods are accessible to all users, including those without biometric-enabled devices or hardware security keys. Additionally, passwordless authentication must be integrated with existing identity management systems and security policies to ensure a smooth transition.

Another consideration is backup and recovery mechanisms. If a user loses access to their primary authentication method, such as a lost security key or a broken biometric sensor, they must have alternative ways to regain access. Organizations should implement backup authentication options, such as trusted device registration, account recovery workflows, or emergency access codes, to prevent users from being locked out of their accounts.

The transition to passwordless authentication also requires user education and awareness. Employees and customers must understand how passwordless authentication works and how to use their authentication methods securely. Organizations should provide clear guidelines on enrolling in passwordless authentication, managing authentication devices, and recognizing potential security threats. By fostering a culture of security awareness, organizations can ensure a successful adoption of passwordless authentication.

Regulatory compliance is another factor driving the adoption of passwordless authentication. Regulations such as GDPR, HIPAA, and PSD2 require organizations to implement strong authentication mechanisms to protect sensitive data. Passwordless authentication aligns with these compliance requirements by reducing the risk of credential-based attacks and enhancing identity security. By integrating passwordless authentication into their IAM frameworks, organizations can meet regulatory standards while improving user experience.

As identity threats continue to evolve, passwordless authentication is becoming the preferred approach for securing digital access. By eliminating passwords and leveraging strong authentication methods, organizations can enhance security, reduce friction for users, and improve overall identity management. As more businesses adopt passwordless SSO solutions, the future of authentication will be defined by seamless, secure, and password-free access to digital services.

How Federated Identity Works: A Technical Overview

Federated identity is a system that allows users to authenticate once and access multiple applications across different organizations without needing to create separate credentials for each service. It is a cornerstone of modern identity and access management (IAM), enabling seamless authentication while maintaining security and user convenience. Federated identity is built on trust relationships between identity providers (IdPs) and service providers (SPs), allowing authentication tokens to be exchanged securely between different domains. The technical implementation of federated identity relies on standardized authentication protocols, cryptographic security mechanisms, and identity federation frameworks.

At its core, federated identity works by externalizing authentication to a trusted identity provider. Instead of an application handling authentication itself, it redirects users to an IdP, which verifies their identity and issues an authentication token. The application, acting as a service provider, then validates the token and grants access to the user. This approach decouples authentication from individual applications, reducing the need for users to maintain multiple sets of credentials and improving security by centralizing identity verification.

Federated identity is implemented using several authentication and authorization protocols, including Security Assertion Markup Language (SAML), OAuth 2.0, and OpenID Connect (OIDC). These protocols standardize how identity data is exchanged between IdPs and SPs, ensuring interoperability across different systems and organizations.

SAML is an XML-based protocol primarily used in enterprise environments to enable Single Sign-On (SSO). It defines how authentication assertions are created and transmitted between IdPs and SPs. In a typical SAML authentication flow, a user attempts to access an SP, which redirects them to the IdP for authentication. The IdP verifies the user's credentials and issues a SAML assertion, which is a digitally signed document containing identity attributes and authentication details. The assertion is sent back to the SP, which validates its signature and grants access if the assertion is trusted.

OAuth 2.0, in contrast, is an authorization framework designed to grant applications limited access to user resources without exposing credentials. While OAuth 2.0 does not provide authentication by itself, it is often used in federated identity scenarios to delegate access. When combined with OpenID Connect, OAuth 2.0 can be extended to handle authentication as well. OpenID Connect adds an ID token to OAuth 2.0's authorization flow, allowing applications to verify user identities. Unlike SAML, which relies on XML, OpenID Connect uses JSON Web Tokens (JWTs), making it more lightweight and suitable for modern web and mobile applications.

The process of federated authentication begins with the establishment of a trust relationship between the IdP and the SP. This is typically achieved through the exchange of federation metadata, which contains details such as entity identifiers, cryptographic keys, and endpoint URLs. The metadata ensures that both parties can securely communicate and validate authentication tokens. Trust is maintained using public-key cryptography, where authentication assertions are digitally signed by the IdP using a private key, and the SP verifies the signature using the corresponding public key.

When a user attempts to authenticate through a federated identity system, their authentication request follows a well-defined sequence of interactions. First, the user accesses an SP and is redirected to the IdP for authentication. The IdP presents a login page where the user enters their credentials. If the credentials are valid, the IdP issues an authentication token, which is sent back to the SP either through an HTTP redirect or a back-channel request. The SP validates the token's integrity, extracts user identity attributes, and grants access accordingly.

A key advantage of federated identity is Single Sign-On (SSO), which allows users to log in once and access multiple applications without re-authenticating. Once a user is authenticated by an IdP, they can seamlessly access other federated services without being prompted for credentials again. This is achieved through session management techniques, such as browser cookies and token-based authentication, which track the user's authentication state across different applications.

Security is a critical consideration in federated identity implementations. Because authentication is centralized, an IdP breach could compromise multiple applications relying on it for identity verification. To mitigate this risk, organizations must implement strong authentication mechanisms, such as multi-factor authentication (MFA), to ensure that even if passwords are compromised, unauthorized access remains difficult. Additionally, federated identity providers should enforce strict token expiration policies and monitor authentication logs for anomalies.

Another security concern is token interception and replay attacks, where an attacker captures an authentication token and reuses it to gain unauthorized access. To prevent this, federated identity systems use signed and encrypted tokens, enforce HTTPS for secure transmission, and implement nonce and timestamp validation to ensure that tokens cannot be reused. In OpenID Connect, PKCE (Proof Key for Code Exchange) adds an additional layer of protection against code interception attacks in public clients such as mobile and single-page applications.

Federated identity is widely used in enterprise environments, cloud services, and government frameworks. In corporate settings, it enables employees to authenticate with their corporate credentials and access third-party applications such as Google Workspace, Salesforce, and AWS without managing separate passwords. Many organizations integrate their on-premises Active Directory with cloud-based identity providers using federation bridges, such as Microsoft Entra ID (formerly Azure AD), to extend authentication across hybrid environments.

In the public sector, federated identity enables secure citizen authentication for government services. Many countries implement national identity providers that allow citizens to use a single authentication system for accessing tax services, healthcare portals, and social security systems. This reduces the complexity of managing multiple credentials and enhances the security of public sector applications.

Federated identity is also crucial in academic and research institutions, where students and faculty members need access to shared resources across different universities and research organizations. Initiatives like eduGAIN and InCommon provide federated authentication frameworks that allow users to access academic databases, online learning platforms, and research collaboration tools using their institutional credentials.

As organizations continue to adopt cloud computing, hybrid IT environments, and decentralized identity models, federated identity remains a key enabler of secure and scalable authentication. Emerging standards such as Verifiable Credentials (VCs) and Decentralized Identifiers (DIDs) are exploring new ways to enhance federated identity while giving users greater control over their personal data. These advancements aim to improve privacy-preserving authentication, reducing reliance on centralized identity providers and enabling self-sovereign identity.

By implementing federated identity with strong security practices, organizations can streamline authentication, improve user experience, and enhance security across multiple applications and domains. As identity management continues to evolve, federated identity will remain a fundamental component of modern authentication strategies, enabling seamless and secure access to digital services.

Setting Up an Identity Provider (IdP)

An Identity Provider (IdP) is a crucial component in identity and access management (IAM), responsible for authenticating users and issuing identity tokens that allow access to various applications and services. Setting up an IdP correctly ensures a secure and seamless authentication experience while enabling Single Sign-On (SSO), federated identity, and multi-factor authentication (MFA). Organizations implementing an IdP must consider security best practices, compliance requirements, and integration with service providers (SPs) to build a robust identity infrastructure.

The first step in setting up an IdP is choosing the right identity management solution. There are several commercial and open-source IdPs available, including Microsoft Entra ID (formerly Azure AD), Okta, Ping Identity, ForgeRock, Keycloak, and Google Workspace Identity Services. The choice of IdP depends on factors such as existing IT infrastructure, required authentication protocols, scalability needs, and integration with third-party applications. Some organizations prefer cloud-based IdPs, such as Entra ID or Okta, which provide managed identity services, while others opt for on-premises solutions, such as Active Directory Federation Services (AD FS) or Keycloak, for greater control over authentication and user data.

Once an IdP is selected, the next step is deploying and configuring the identity provider. Cloud-based IdPs typically offer a straightforward setup process, with pre-configured integrations for common enterprise applications. On-premises deployments, however, require installing the IdP software on dedicated servers, configuring domain name settings, and securing communication channels using SSL/TLS certificates. A key consideration in this phase is ensuring high availability and redundancy, as the IdP serves as the primary authentication authority. Organizations often deploy multiple IdP instances with load balancing and failover mechanisms to prevent downtime and ensure continuous authentication services.

User directory integration is an essential aspect of IdP configuration. Most IdPs integrate with Lightweight Directory Access Protocol (LDAP) directories, such as Microsoft Active Directory (AD) or OpenLDAP, to authenticate users and retrieve identity attributes. Organizations using a hybrid identity model, where on-premises directories coexist with cloud-based IdPs, may configure directory synchronization tools such as Microsoft Entra Connect to keep user identities updated across environments. This integration allows organizations to leverage existing identity stores while extending authentication capabilities to cloud-based applications.

A critical part of IdP setup is configuring authentication protocols. IdPs support various authentication and authorization protocols, including SAML (Security Assertion Markup Language), OAuth 2.0, OpenID Connect (OIDC), and Kerberos. The choice of protocol depends on the applications and service providers that need to authenticate users.

SAML is widely used for enterprise Single Sign-On (SSO), allowing users to authenticate once and access multiple business applications without re-entering credentials.

OAuth 2.0 is commonly used for API authorization, enabling applications to request access tokens instead of passwords.

OpenID Connect (OIDC) extends OAuth 2.0 by providing authentication capabilities, allowing service providers to verify user identities using JSON Web Tokens (JWTs).

Kerberos is primarily used in on-premises Windows environments, enabling secure authentication within Microsoft Active Directory domains.

Once authentication protocols are configured, the IdP must establish trust relationships with service providers (SPs). This involves exchanging metadata files containing entity identifiers, cryptographic signing certificates, and endpoint URLs. In a federated identity setup, the IdP acts as the trusted authority, issuing signed authentication assertions that SPs validate before granting access. Properly managing trust relationships is crucial to ensuring secure authentication flows and preventing unauthorized access.

To enhance security, organizations should implement Multi-Factor Authentication (MFA) at the IdP level. MFA adds an additional layer of security by requiring users to verify their identity using a second factor, such as one-time passcodes (OTPs), biometric authentication, or security keys. Most IdPs support adaptive authentication, where authentication requirements dynamically adjust based on risk factors, such as login location, device type, and user behavior. Enforcing MFA at the IdP prevents unauthorized access even if passwords are compromised, significantly improving security posture.

Another key security measure is token lifecycle management. IdPs issue authentication tokens that grant access to applications and APIs, but these tokens must be properly managed to prevent security risks. Best practices include:

Setting token expiration times to limit the duration of authentication sessions.

Implementing token revocation mechanisms to allow administrators to invalidate compromised tokens.

Using refresh tokens to enable long-lived authentication without storing passwords on client devices.

Encrypting and signing authentication tokens to ensure their integrity and prevent tampering.

Logging and monitoring authentication events is essential for detecting security threats and maintaining compliance. IdPs generate audit logs that record authentication attempts, failed login attempts, token issuance, and access requests. Organizations should integrate IdP logs with Security Information and Event Management (SIEM) systems to enable real-time threat detection and response. Monitoring tools can identify anomalies, such as repeated login failures, access from unusual locations, or excessive authentication requests, helping security teams mitigate risks before they lead to data breaches.

IdP configuration should also include role-based access control (RBAC) and attribute-based access control (ABAC) policies to enforce access restrictions based on user roles and attributes. By defining group-based policies, organizations can ensure that users only have access to the applications and data necessary for their job functions. Some IdPs also support Just-in-Time (JIT) user provisioning, allowing automatic account creation in service providers when users authenticate for the first time, streamlining user onboarding.

For organizations adopting hybrid and multi-cloud architectures, federation with external IdPs is a key consideration. Many enterprises need to integrate their IdPs with third-party identity providers, such as Google Workspace, AWS IAM, or partner organizations. This is achieved using identity federation standards, such as SAML federation or cross-domain OAuth trust relationships. Federating identities across different organizations enables secure business-to-business (B2B) collaborations, allowing users from partner organizations to authenticate using their own credentials.

As identity security continues to evolve, passwordless authentication is becoming a standard feature in modern IdPs. Many identity providers now support biometric authentication, hardware security keys (FIDO2/WebAuthn), and push notification-based authentication to eliminate the need for passwords. Implementing passwordless authentication at the IdP level enhances security while improving the user experience by reducing password-related friction.

Once the IdP is fully configured and tested, organizations must ensure that disaster recovery and failover mechanisms are in place. Backup IdP instances, geographic redundancy, and failover strategies should be implemented to ensure continuous authentication availability. Regular security audits, penetration testing, and compliance checks should also be conducted to maintain the integrity of the identity infrastructure.

Setting up an Identity Provider is a foundational step in securing enterprise authentication and enabling federated identity management. A well-configured IdP not only enhances security and compliance but also improves user experience by enabling seamless authentication across multiple services. By following best practices, integrating with modern authentication protocols, and adopting security-first principles, organizations can build a robust, scalable, and future-ready identity management system.

Configuring a Service Provider (SP) for Federation

A Service Provider (SP) is an application or system that relies on an Identity Provider (IdP) for authentication in a federated identity environment. Instead of handling user authentication independently, the SP delegates authentication to a trusted IdP, which verifies user credentials and issues authentication assertions. Configuring an SP for federation is a critical step in enabling Single Sign-On (SSO), improving security, and providing a seamless authentication experience for users accessing multiple services. Proper configuration ensures that authentication flows are secure, identity attributes are mapped correctly, and trust relationships between the SP and IdP are properly established.

The first step in configuring an SP is choosing the appropriate federation protocol to integrate with the IdP. The most commonly used protocols for federated authentication include Security Assertion Markup Language (SAML), OpenID Connect (OIDC), and OAuth 2.0.

SAML is widely used in enterprise environments and enables SSO by exchanging authentication assertions between the IdP and SP using XML-based messages.

OpenID Connect (OIDC) is built on top of OAuth 2.0 and uses JSON Web Tokens (JWTs) to provide authentication, making it a more lightweight and modern alternative to SAML.

OAuth 2.0 is primarily used for authorization, allowing an SP to request access tokens to call APIs on behalf of an authenticated user.

Once the appropriate protocol is chosen, the next step is establishing trust between the SP and IdP. This is done by exchanging federation metadata, which contains information such as entity identifiers, endpoint URLs, and cryptographic signing certificates. The SP must import the IdP's metadata file or manually configure Issuer URLs, Single Sign-On (SSO) endpoints, and public certificates to validate authentication responses. Similarly, the IdP must be configured to recognize the SP and issue authentication assertions accordingly.

With the trust relationship established, the SP must define authentication request settings to specify how users will authenticate. For SAML-based authentication, the SP typically sends an AuthnRequest to the IdP, requesting authentication for a user. The binding method used to send authentication requests can be either HTTP-Redirect Binding (which redirects the user to the IdP via URL parameters) or HTTP-POST Binding (which sends authentication requests using an HTML form post). For OpenID Connect, authentication requests are sent as OAuth 2.0 authorization requests, specifying scopes and response types to define what user attributes should be returned.

Handling authentication responses is a crucial part of SP configuration. When a user successfully authenticates with the IdP, the IdP issues an authentication assertion (in SAML) or an ID token (in OpenID Connect) that must be validated by the SP. The SP must check the following:

Signature verification: The authentication assertion must be signed using the IdP's public certificate to ensure integrity and authenticity.

Token expiration: The validity of the assertion or token should be checked to prevent replay attacks.

Audience restriction: The assertion or token should be intended for the SP and not for another service.

Attribute mapping: Identity attributes (such as username, email, and group membership) should be extracted and mapped correctly to the SP's user model.

Attribute mapping is an important aspect of configuring an SP, as it determines how user identity information is handled within the application. The IdP sends attributes such as User ID, email, display name, roles, and group membership, which must be mapped to the corresponding fields in the SP's user directory. Some IdPs allow attribute transformations, such as normalizing email addresses or assigning default roles based on predefined rules. The SP must be configured to process these attributes correctly to ensure seamless user provisioning and access control.

SPs must also define authorization policies based on the identity attributes received from the IdP. For example, if an SP receives a group membership claim, it can enforce role-based access control (RBAC) by granting different levels of access based on the user's group assignments. Some SPs also support attribute-based access control (ABAC), where access decisions are made dynamically based on user attributes, such as location, department, or authentication method.

To improve security, SPs should enforce session management policies to handle user authentication states effectively. A common approach is Single Logout (SLO), where a user who logs out of one SP is automatically logged out of all federated services. SLO can be implemented using SAML Logout Requests or OpenID Connect End-Session Endpoints, ensuring that session termination is synchronized across all connected services. Additionally, SPs should configure token revocation mechanisms to invalidate authentication tokens if a user session is terminated or a security breach is detected.

Another security best practice is implementing Multi-Factor Authentication (MFA) policies in collaboration with the IdP. Some

IdPs enforce adaptive authentication, which dynamically prompts for MFA based on user risk factors such as login location, device type, or behavior anomalies. The SP should be configured to respect these authentication policies and require additional verification steps when needed.

Logging and monitoring authentication events is essential for detecting security threats and maintaining compliance. SPs should generate audit logs that record authentication attempts, failed login attempts, and access requests. Integrating authentication logs with Security Information and Event Management (SIEM) systems allows organizations to detect suspicious activity, such as unauthorized access attempts or unusual login patterns. Some SPs also support real-time alerting and automated incident response, helping security teams mitigate threats proactively.

For cloud-based applications, integrating an SP with cloud identity providers such as Microsoft Entra ID, Okta, or Google Workspace enables organizations to extend authentication capabilities across SaaS applications. Many cloud platforms offer pre-configured SP templates that simplify the integration process, allowing administrators to enable federated authentication with minimal manual configuration. Cloud SPs must also implement OAuth 2.0 token validation and ensure compliance with cloud security best practices.

Hybrid identity environments, where organizations operate a mix of on-premises and cloud applications, require special considerations for SP configuration. Many enterprises integrate their on-premises Active Directory Federation Services (AD FS) with cloud identity providers to enable seamless authentication for both internal and external applications. In such cases, SPs must be configured to accept authentication assertions from both on-premises IdPs and cloud IdPs, ensuring consistent access policies across all environments.

Testing and validating the SP configuration is a critical final step before deploying federated authentication in a production environment. Administrators should conduct comprehensive integration tests, verifying that authentication requests and responses are correctly processed, attributes are mapped accurately, and access policies function as expected. Using SAML Tracer, OAuth Debugger, or

OpenID Connect validation tools can help diagnose authentication issues and ensure proper protocol compliance. Organizations should also perform penetration testing and security audits to identify vulnerabilities in their federated authentication setup.

Properly configuring a Service Provider for federation ensures that authentication flows are secure, scalable, and user-friendly. By following best practices, integrating security controls, and maintaining continuous monitoring, organizations can enable a trusted federated identity ecosystem that enhances security while providing seamless access to digital services.

Federation Metadata: What It Is and Why It Matters

Federation metadata is a critical component in federated identity management, serving as a structured document that facilitates secure communication between an Identity Provider (IdP) and a Service Provider (SP). This metadata file contains essential configuration details that allow federated entities to establish trust, exchange authentication tokens, and ensure interoperability across different authentication systems. By automating the configuration process and reducing the risk of misconfigurations, federation metadata simplifies identity federation while enhancing security and reliability.

At its core, federation metadata is an XML document that includes information about an IdP or SP, such as entity identifiers, public keys, supported authentication protocols, and endpoint URLs. It acts as a digital contract, defining how authentication requests and responses should be exchanged between federated entities. Instead of manually configuring authentication parameters, administrators can use metadata files to streamline integration, ensuring that both parties follow a common set of security and communication rules.

One of the primary components of federation metadata is the Entity ID, a unique identifier that distinguishes the IdP or SP within a federated environment. This identifier ensures that authentication assertions and tokens are issued and accepted by the correct entities. Without a properly defined Entity ID, authentication requests could be misdirected or fail due to mismatched configurations.

Another key element in federation metadata is the Single Sign-On (SSO) endpoints, which specify the URLs used for authentication requests, responses, and logout processes. For an IdP, these endpoints define where users should be redirected to authenticate, while for an SP, they indicate where authentication responses should be sent. Ensuring the correct configuration of these endpoints is crucial for enabling seamless authentication workflows and preventing session disruptions.

Federation metadata also includes public keys and digital signatures, which are essential for securing authentication assertions. In a federated environment, IdPs sign authentication responses using their private keys, and SPs validate these signatures using the corresponding public keys found in the metadata file. This cryptographic mechanism prevents tampering, ensuring that authentication assertions cannot be modified or forged by malicious actors. Similarly, SPs may sign authentication requests to verify their authenticity before sending them to the IdP.

The metadata document defines supported authentication protocols, such as SAML (Security Assertion Markup Language), OpenID Connect (OIDC), and OAuth 2.0. This ensures that both the IdP and SP can communicate using compatible protocols, avoiding interoperability issues. Some metadata files also specify additional security policies, such as required encryption algorithms, session timeout settings, and token expiration policies. By standardizing these security parameters, federation metadata helps maintain a consistent level of protection across federated systems.

One of the main advantages of using federation metadata is its ability to automate the federation setup process. Instead of manually configuring trust relationships, administrators can simply import the metadata file from a trusted partner. Many identity providers and service providers support metadata auto-refresh, allowing them to periodically fetch updated metadata files to reflect changes such as new cryptographic keys or endpoint modifications. This automation reduces administrative overhead and minimizes the risk of authentication failures caused by outdated configurations.

Security is a critical aspect of federation metadata management. Since metadata files contain sensitive information, they must be secured against tampering and unauthorized access. Best practices include:

Hosting metadata files over HTTPS to prevent interception or manipulation.

Digitally signing metadata files to ensure integrity and authenticity.

Regularly rotating encryption keys to maintain security resilience.

Restricting access to metadata endpoints to prevent unauthorized modifications.

Another important consideration is metadata lifecycle management, ensuring that metadata remains up to date as identity systems evolve. Organizations should establish processes for regularly updating metadata, especially when encryption keys are rotated, authentication endpoints change, or new security policies are implemented. Failure to update metadata in a timely manner can lead to authentication errors, broken federations, and potential security vulnerabilities.

Federation metadata plays a crucial role in multi-organization federations, such as those used in higher education, healthcare, and government identity frameworks. For example, academic federations like eduGAIN and InCommon rely on federation metadata to establish trust relationships between universities and research institutions, enabling students and faculty members to access shared resources using their institutional credentials. Similarly, government identity frameworks use federation metadata to enable secure citizen authentication across multiple agencies, ensuring interoperability between different identity providers.

For cloud-based identity providers, federation metadata is particularly valuable in hybrid identity environments, where organizations integrate on-premises directories with cloud services. By exchanging metadata between Active Directory Federation Services (AD FS), Microsoft Entra ID (formerly Azure AD), Okta, and Google Workspace, organizations can enable secure federated authentication across both cloud and on-premises applications. This simplifies identity synchronization, reduces password fatigue, and enhances security by enforcing centralized authentication policies.

In enterprise SSO implementations, federation metadata is used to integrate corporate applications with external identity providers. Many SaaS applications, such as Salesforce, ServiceNow, and AWS IAM, support SAML-based SSO and allow administrators to import federation metadata directly into their configuration settings. This integration streamlines the authentication process, enabling employees to access multiple applications with a single login while maintaining strong authentication controls.

As identity and access management (IAM) continues to evolve, metadata-driven federation is becoming increasingly important for ensuring scalable and secure authentication. Emerging standards, such as Verifiable Credentials (VCs) and Decentralized Identifiers (DIDs), are exploring new ways to enhance identity federation while reducing reliance on centralized identity providers. These technologies aim to provide self-sovereign identity (SSI), allowing users to control their digital identities while still leveraging federation metadata for authentication interoperability.

Organizations implementing federated authentication must adopt best practices for managing federation metadata, including:

Regular metadata validation to detect expired certificates, incorrect endpoints, or missing attributes.

Automated metadata updates to minimize manual configuration efforts and prevent authentication failures.

Security reviews of metadata configurations to identify potential vulnerabilities or misconfigurations.

Documenting metadata dependencies to ensure continuity in case of identity provider migrations or infrastructure changes.

By effectively managing federation metadata, organizations can enhance security, simplify identity integration, and ensure reliable authentication across federated services. Whether for enterprise SSO, academic federations, cloud identity integration, or government identity frameworks, federation metadata remains a fundamental component in the future of identity and access management.

Implementing SAML-Based SSO in an Enterprise Environment

Security Assertion Markup Language (SAML) is one of the most widely used protocols for implementing Single Sign-On (SSO) in enterprise environments. By enabling users to authenticate once and access multiple applications without needing to log in repeatedly, SAML-based SSO enhances security, improves user experience, and reduces the administrative burden associated with managing credentials. Enterprises use SAML to integrate identity providers (IdPs) with service providers (SPs), ensuring seamless authentication while enforcing strong security controls.

Implementing SAML-based SSO begins with defining the trust relationship between the identity provider and the service provider. The IdP is responsible for authenticating users and issuing SAML assertions, while the SP relies on these assertions to grant access to applications. This trust relationship is established through the exchange of federation metadata, which contains details such as entity identifiers, authentication endpoints, and cryptographic signing certificates. Proper configuration of metadata ensures secure communication and prevents authentication failures due to mismatched configurations.

One of the key components of SAML-based SSO is the SAML assertion, which serves as the authentication token that the IdP sends to the SP. A SAML assertion consists of three main elements:

Authentication statement: Confirms that the user has been authenticated by the IdP at a specific time using a particular method, such as password-based authentication or multi-factor authentication (MFA).

Attribute statement: Contains user identity attributes, such as username, email, roles, or group memberships, which the SP can use to determine authorization levels.

Authorization decision statement: Specifies whether the user is permitted to access the requested resource based on predefined access policies.

When a user attempts to access an enterprise application integrated with SAML-based SSO, the authentication flow follows a well-defined sequence. First, the user attempts to log into the SP. The SP, recognizing that authentication is handled by an external IdP, generates a SAML authentication request and redirects the user to the IdP's login page. The user enters their credentials, and the IdP verifies their identity. Upon successful authentication, the IdP generates a SAML response containing the SAML assertion and digitally signs it to ensure integrity. The response is then sent back to the SP via an HTTP-POST binding or HTTP-Redirect binding, where it is validated, and the user is granted access to the application.

Security plays a crucial role in SAML-based SSO implementations. Since SAML assertions serve as authentication tokens, they must be protected against interception and tampering. One of the primary security mechanisms used in SAML is digital signatures. The IdP signs SAML assertions using its private key, and the SP verifies the signature using the IdP's public key found in the federation metadata. This prevents unauthorized modification of authentication assertions by attackers attempting to gain unauthorized access.

Encryption is another important security feature. While signing ensures the authenticity of SAML assertions, encryption protects the sensitive data within them. In high-security environments, enterprises configure SAML assertions to be encrypted so that even if an assertion is intercepted, its contents remain unreadable without the appropriate decryption keys. The SP decrypts the assertion using its private key before processing the authentication response.

Enterprises must also consider token expiration policies when implementing SAML-based SSO. To prevent replay attacks, where an attacker captures and reuses a valid authentication response, SAML assertions include timestamps that indicate their validity period. The SP must enforce strict validation of assertion timestamps, rejecting expired or replayed assertions. Additionally, session timeouts should be configured to automatically log out inactive users, reducing the risk of unauthorized access.

Attribute mapping is another critical aspect of SAML-based SSO integration. The IdP provides user identity attributes within the SAML assertion, but different service providers may require different attribute formats. Enterprises must ensure that attributes such as email, username, and group membership are correctly mapped between the IdP and SP. Some IdPs allow attribute transformation, enabling organizations to modify attribute values before sending them to the SP. Proper attribute mapping ensures seamless user provisioning and access control enforcement.

Another important feature in SAML-based SSO is Single Logout (SLO). When a user logs out of one application, SLO ensures that they are also logged out of all other federated applications. This prevents session persistence across multiple services, reducing security risks associated with open sessions. SLO is implemented using SAML Logout Requests, which notify the IdP and other SPs that the user session should be terminated. Proper SLO configuration is crucial in enterprise environments where users access multiple applications throughout the day.

Integrating SAML-based SSO with multi-factor authentication (MFA) further enhances security. While SAML itself does not define specific MFA methods, IdPs can enforce additional authentication factors before issuing SAML assertions. This is particularly useful in enterprises that require adaptive authentication, where users must provide additional verification if they attempt to log in from an unknown location, device, or network. By combining SAML with MFA, organizations can strengthen authentication while maintaining a frictionless user experience.

Monitoring and logging are essential for maintaining the security and integrity of SAML-based SSO implementations. Enterprises should configure their IdPs and SPs to generate audit logs that record authentication attempts, failed logins, token validation errors, and access requests. These logs should be integrated with Security Information and Event Management (SIEM) systems, allowing real-time monitoring and alerting of suspicious authentication activity. Detecting anomalies, such as repeated failed authentication attempts or authentication from unusual locations, helps organizations proactively respond to potential security threats.

For organizations operating in hybrid cloud environments, integrating SAML-based SSO with cloud identity providers enables seamless authentication across on-premises and cloud applications. Solutions such as Microsoft Entra ID (Azure AD), Okta, and Google Workspace Identity provide pre-configured SAML integrations for enterprise applications, simplifying the deployment process. Hybrid identity environments require proper synchronization of user directories, ensuring that on-premises Active Directory (AD) identities are mapped correctly to cloud-based IdPs for seamless authentication.

Testing and validation are critical before deploying SAML-based SSO in a production environment. Enterprises should conduct integration testing using tools such as SAML Tracer or SAML Validator to verify authentication flows, assertion integrity, and attribute mappings. End-to-end user testing should also be performed to ensure that employees can log in successfully and access authorized resources without authentication failures. By validating SAML configurations before deployment, organizations can minimize disruptions and ensure a smooth transition to federated authentication.

A well-implemented SAML-based SSO solution provides enterprises with a scalable, secure, and efficient authentication framework. By configuring strong authentication policies, ensuring proper encryption, implementing session management, and continuously monitoring authentication activity, organizations can maximize the benefits of federated identity while protecting user identities from emerging security threats.

Integrating OAuth 2.0 and OpenID Connect in Web Applications

OAuth 2.0 and OpenID Connect (OIDC) are two of the most widely used authentication and authorization protocols in modern web applications. OAuth 2.0 provides a framework for granting applications delegated access to user resources without exposing passwords, while OpenID Connect extends OAuth 2.0 to include authentication capabilities, allowing applications to verify a user's identity. Together, these protocols enable secure authentication and authorization workflows, making them essential for integrating Single Sign-On (SSO) and identity federation in web applications.

The integration of OAuth 2.0 and OpenID Connect begins with understanding their roles in a web application. OAuth 2.0 is primarily designed for authorization, allowing third-party applications to request access to a user's protected resources, such as APIs or cloud services, on their behalf. It defines four primary roles: the resource owner (the user), the client (the application requesting access), the authorization server (which issues access tokens), and the resource server (which validates access tokens and grants access to protected resources).

OpenID Connect builds on top of OAuth 2.0 by introducing an ID token, which is a JSON Web Token (JWT) that contains identity claims about the authenticated user. This allows applications to authenticate users securely and retrieve user attributes, such as email, name, and roles, without needing to manage credentials directly. OpenID Connect also defines an authentication flow, where the application redirects the user to an identity provider (IdP), such as Google, Microsoft Entra ID, or Okta, for authentication. Once authenticated, the IdP issues an ID token, which the application verifies to establish the user's identity.

When integrating OAuth 2.0 and OpenID Connect in a web application, the first step is selecting an authentication flow that aligns with the application's architecture. The authorization code flow is the most secure and widely used method, particularly for web applications with backend servers. This flow involves the application redirecting the user to the authorization server, where they authenticate and grant permissions. Upon successful authentication, the authorization server issues an authorization code, which the application exchanges for access and ID tokens. By keeping tokens on the backend and using server-side validation, the authorization code flow minimizes the risk of exposing sensitive credentials.

For single-page applications (SPAs) and mobile applications, the authorization code flow with Proof Key for Code Exchange (PKCE) is recommended. PKCE enhances security by requiring the application to generate a code verifier and a code challenge during the initial authentication request. When exchanging the authorization code for tokens, the application must provide the correct code verifier, preventing attackers from intercepting and reusing authorization codes. This approach is particularly useful for JavaScript-based web applications that lack a secure backend for handling secret keys.

Once authentication is complete, the web application must validate the received ID token to ensure its authenticity. ID tokens in OpenID Connect are JWTs signed by the identity provider. The application must verify the signature using the provider's public key, check the issuer (iss) claim to ensure the token came from a trusted IdP, and validate the expiration (exp) claim to confirm that the token is still valid. Token validation can be done using OpenID Connect libraries, such as jwt-decode for JavaScript or PyJWT for Python.

After successful authentication, the application can retrieve user identity attributes from the ID token. OpenID Connect defines standard scopes, such as openid, profile, and email, which determine the attributes included in the token. Additional user attributes can be obtained by requesting specific claims or by making an authenticated request to the UserInfo endpoint provided by the IdP. Applications should carefully manage and store user attributes to enforce role-based access control (RBAC) or attribute-based access control (ABAC).

For applications that need to access APIs on behalf of the user, OAuth 2.0 provides access tokens, which authorize API requests without requiring the user's credentials. The application includes the access token in the Authorization header when making API requests. The resource server validates the token against the authorization server before granting access. Since access tokens have a limited lifespan, applications must implement token refresh mechanisms using refresh tokens, which allow them to obtain new access tokens without requiring the user to reauthenticate.

Security is a critical aspect of OAuth 2.0 and OpenID Connect integration. Since tokens are used to grant access to user resources, they must be protected against leakage and misuse. Access tokens should be stored securely, preferably in HTTP-only cookies rather than local storage, to prevent cross-site scripting (XSS) attacks. Additionally, applications should implement token revocation mechanisms to allow users to revoke access if their credentials are compromised.

To enhance security further, multi-factor authentication (MFA) can be enforced at the identity provider level. Many IdPs support adaptive authentication, which prompts users for additional verification factors, such as a one-time passcode or biometric authentication, when logging in from untrusted devices or locations. By integrating OAuth 2.0 and OpenID Connect with MFA, applications can strengthen authentication security while minimizing friction for trusted users.

For web applications that need federated authentication, integrating OAuth 2.0 and OpenID Connect with an external IdP enables seamless SSO across multiple services. Organizations often configure identity federation with providers such as Microsoft Entra ID, Okta, or Auth0, allowing employees or customers to authenticate using their existing credentials. This eliminates the need for users to create new accounts while maintaining centralized identity management and security policies.

Logging and monitoring are essential for maintaining the security and reliability of OAuth 2.0 and OpenID Connect integrations. Applications should log authentication events, token exchanges, and API access requests to detect unauthorized access attempts or anomalies. Security monitoring tools, such as Security Information and Event Management (SIEM) systems, can help analyze logs and generate alerts for potential security threats.

For applications operating in multi-cloud or hybrid environments, OAuth 2.0 and OpenID Connect enable seamless authentication across different cloud platforms and on-premises systems. Enterprises using hybrid identity architectures can integrate OpenID Connect with Active Directory Federation Services (AD FS) or other on-premises identity providers to extend authentication across internal and external applications. This ensures that employees and partners can securely access resources regardless of their location.

Testing and validating OAuth 2.0 and OpenID Connect configurations is crucial before deployment. Developers should use OAuth debugging tools such as jwt.io, OpenID Connect Playground, and Postman to inspect tokens, verify claims, and troubleshoot authentication flows. By conducting rigorous security testing, organizations can identify and resolve vulnerabilities before exposing authentication endpoints to the public.

OAuth 2.0 and OpenID Connect have become the de facto standards for modern web authentication and authorization. By implementing these protocols correctly, web applications can provide secure, scalable, and user-friendly authentication experiences, reducing reliance on passwords while enabling seamless Single Sign-On, federated identity, and API authorization.

User Provisioning and Deprovisioning in Federated Identity

User provisioning and deprovisioning are critical processes in federated identity management, ensuring that users are granted appropriate access to resources when they join an organization and that their access is revoked when they leave or change roles. In a federated identity environment, these processes must be automated and securely managed across multiple identity providers (IdPs) and service providers (SPs). Effective provisioning and deprovisioning minimize security risks, reduce administrative overhead, and improve compliance with access control policies.

Provisioning in federated identity involves creating and maintaining user accounts across multiple systems based on identity data from a central identity provider. When a new employee, contractor, or partner joins an organization, their identity must be provisioned to various applications and services they need to perform their job. This process typically involves creating a user profile, assigning access roles, synchronizing identity attributes, and ensuring that authentication mechanisms such as single sign-on (SSO) and multi-factor authentication (MFA) are properly configured.

Federated identity provisioning relies on identity federation protocols such as SAML (Security Assertion Markup Language), OpenID Connect (OIDC), and OAuth 2.0, which allow identity information to be exchanged between trusted entities. However, provisioning itself is not handled by these protocols directly. Instead, organizations use Just-in-Time (JIT) provisioning or System for Cross-domain Identity Management (SCIM) to automate the process.

Just-in-Time provisioning occurs when a user attempts to access a service provider for the first time through an identity federation. Instead of manually creating an account in advance, the SP dynamically creates the user account at the time of authentication based on the identity attributes received from the IdP. This approach reduces administrative effort and ensures that users can access applications immediately without requiring prior setup. However, JIT provisioning has limitations, as it does not support user updates, role changes, or deprovisioning, requiring additional synchronization mechanisms.

SCIM is an industry-standard protocol designed to automate user provisioning and deprovisioning across different identity systems. SCIM allows IdPs to synchronize user attributes with service providers in a structured and standardized way, ensuring that changes in the identity directory are propagated to all connected applications. For example, when an employee's department or job title changes, SCIM updates their access permissions accordingly across multiple services, eliminating the need for manual updates. SCIM also enables bulk provisioning, making it easier to onboard large numbers of users at once.

Role-based access control (RBAC) plays a crucial role in user provisioning, ensuring that users are granted the appropriate level of access based on their job responsibilities. In a federated identity system, access rights are often determined by identity attributes such as department, job role, or security clearance. When provisioning users, the IdP assigns them to predefined access groups or roles, which dictate what applications and resources they can access. Organizations may also implement attribute-based access control (ABAC), where access decisions are dynamically determined based on contextual factors such as location, device type, or authentication strength.

User deprovisioning is equally important in federated identity management, ensuring that users no longer have access to resources when they leave the organization or no longer require certain permissions. Deprovisioning is a key security measure to prevent orphaned accounts, which can be exploited by malicious actors to gain unauthorized access. In a federated environment, deprovisioning must be handled efficiently across multiple service providers to avoid security gaps.

Manual deprovisioning, where IT administrators manually disable or delete accounts, is not scalable in large enterprises. Instead, automated deprovisioning mechanisms ensure that user accounts are disabled or revoked as soon as an employee departs. SCIM supports automatic deprovisioning, allowing identity providers to communicate user status changes to all linked service providers. When a user is marked as inactive or removed from the corporate directory, SCIM ensures that the deprovisioning action is propagated to all connected applications.

Account disablement and deletion are two different approaches to deprovisioning. Disabling an account temporarily prevents a user from logging in but retains their account data, which can be useful for compliance or auditing purposes. Deleting an account removes all associated data, ensuring that the user's credentials cannot be reused. Organizations must define policies for determining when accounts should be disabled versus deleted, considering factors such as regulatory retention requirements, re-hiring scenarios, and security risks.

Security and compliance are critical concerns in user provisioning and deprovisioning. Many regulations, such as GDPR, HIPAA, and SOC 2, require organizations to enforce strict access controls and ensure that user access is properly managed. Auditing and logging are essential for tracking who has been provisioned, what access they have, and when their access is revoked. Organizations should integrate provisioning and deprovisioning logs with Security Information and Event Management (SIEM) systems to detect anomalies, such as unauthorized provisioning or failure to revoke access for terminated users.

Multi-tenancy and external user provisioning introduce additional challenges in federated identity management. Many organizations must manage access for contractors, partners, or external customers, whose access requirements differ from internal employees. In such cases, organizations often implement identity governance policies, requiring periodic access reviews and re-certification of permissions. Automated tools can help enforce least privilege access, ensuring that users only retain access to necessary resources and that access is revoked when no longer needed.

Lifecycle management in federated identity goes beyond provisioning and deprovisioning. Organizations must also account for access transitions, such as role changes, promotions, or internal transfers. A user moving from one department to another may require new access permissions while losing access to their previous department's resources. Automated identity lifecycle management (ILM) solutions can help synchronize these changes across federated systems, reducing the risk of excessive privileges or unauthorized access.

Another consideration in federated provisioning is handling inactive accounts. Some users, particularly contractors or seasonal employees, may require periodic access to systems but remain inactive for extended periods. Organizations should implement automated inactivity policies that deactivate accounts after a specified duration and require reactivation through identity verification. This reduces the risk of dormant accounts being exploited by attackers.

Testing and validating provisioning workflows is a crucial step in federated identity deployments. Organizations should conduct pilot programs before rolling out automated provisioning and deprovisioning at scale. Using test accounts, administrators can verify that role assignments, attribute mappings, and deprovisioning rules work as expected. Continuous monitoring and improvement ensure that provisioning processes remain efficient and aligned with business and security requirements.

A well-implemented user provisioning and deprovisioning strategy in federated identity environments ensures that access is granted and revoked efficiently, security risks are minimized, and compliance requirements are met. By leveraging SCIM, Just-in-Time provisioning, role-based access controls, and automated lifecycle management, organizations can streamline identity management while protecting their digital assets from unauthorized access.

Attribute Mapping and Claims Transformation

Attribute mapping and claims transformation are essential components of identity federation and Single Sign-On (SSO) implementations. These processes ensure that identity attributes exchanged between an Identity Provider (IdP) and a Service Provider (SP) are correctly interpreted, formatted, and applied to enforce authentication and authorization policies. In federated identity systems, different applications and organizations may use distinct attribute naming conventions and data formats, requiring transformations to achieve interoperability. Properly mapping attributes and transforming claims allows seamless user authentication while enforcing security policies and role-based access control (RBAC).

In identity federation, attributes are pieces of identity information that describe a user, such as username, email address, first name, last name, department, and role. These attributes are sent from the IdP to the SP as part of an authentication token, which may be a SAML assertion, an OAuth 2.0 access token, or an OpenID Connect (OIDC) ID token. The SP relies on these attributes to create user sessions, determine access levels, and enforce security policies. However, different service providers may require attributes in specific formats, necessitating attribute mapping to align identity data with application requirements.

Claims transformation extends attribute mapping by modifying attribute values before passing them to the service provider. Claims refer to the identity-related statements asserted by the IdP, such as user roles, group memberships, or authentication methods used. A claims transformation engine processes these statements, applying modifications such as renaming attributes, formatting values, aggregating multiple attributes, or applying conditional logic based on predefined rules. These transformations ensure that identity data conforms to the structure expected by the SP.

One of the most common attribute mapping challenges arises when the IdP and SP use different naming conventions for the same identity attribute. For example, an IdP may provide the user's email address under the attribute name mail, while the SP expects it as email. Without proper mapping, the SP would fail to recognize the attribute, potentially causing authentication failures or incorrect user provisioning. Administrators must configure attribute mappings in the IdP or SP to translate mail to email during authentication exchanges.

Claims transformation also plays a crucial role in role-based access control (RBAC). Many applications rely on role-based permissions to grant or restrict access to specific resources. An IdP may store user roles as group memberships (memberOf=HRGroup), while an SP expects a role attribute such as role=HRAdmin. A claims transformation rule can translate group memberships into appropriate role attributes by applying a mapping such as:

If memberOf=HRGroup, then role=HRAdmin.

If memberOf=FinanceGroup, then role=FinanceUser.

This approach ensures that users receive correct role assignments across different applications, preventing privilege escalation or access denials due to mismatched role formats.

Another common use case for claims transformation is normalizing identity attributes. Organizations often integrate multiple identity sources, such as Active Directory, LDAP, or cloud-based identity providers, each using different formats for identity data. For example, some systems may store usernames in uppercase (JDOE), while others require lowercase (jdoe). A claims transformation rule can convert all usernames to lowercase before sending them to the SP, ensuring consistency and avoiding authentication errors.

Claims transformation also enables attribute filtering, where only specific identity attributes are passed to the SP to protect user privacy. Some service providers may request excessive user information, such as phone numbers or home addresses, which are unnecessary for authentication. By configuring attribute filtering rules, administrators can restrict claims to only those required by the SP, improving data minimization and compliance with privacy regulations such as GDPR and CCPA.

Organizations implementing multi-factor authentication (MFA) can use claims transformation to enforce authentication policies dynamically. An IdP can include an authentication method reference claim (acr) indicating whether the user authenticated using MFA or a weaker authentication method. An SP can then enforce security policies based on this claim, such as:

If acr=mfa, grant full access.

If acr=password, require additional verification before accessing sensitive data.

This mechanism ensures that applications enforce appropriate security controls based on the strength of authentication, reducing the risk of unauthorized access.

Federated identity environments often require conditional attribute transformations based on user attributes or authentication context. For example, a multinational organization may need to enforce regional access policies, mapping country codes to specific attributes:

If country=US, then region=NorthAmerica.

If country=FR, then region=Europe.

By dynamically transforming attributes based on contextual rules, organizations can implement fine-grained access control policies tailored to their business needs.

When integrating with cloud-based service providers, administrators must often transform claims to comply with application-specific requirements. Many cloud platforms, such as Microsoft Entra ID (formerly Azure AD), Okta, and Google Workspace, provide built-in claim transformation engines that allow administrators to modify attribute mappings through graphical interfaces or policy scripting languages. These tools enable organizations to create custom rules for claims processing, simplifying integration with third-party applications.

Security considerations are essential when performing attribute mapping and claims transformation. If attributes are improperly mapped or transformed, users may receive incorrect access permissions, leading to security vulnerabilities. Attribute injection attacks, where an attacker manipulates identity attributes to gain elevated privileges, can occur if claims transformation rules are misconfigured. To mitigate these risks, organizations should:

Validate attribute mappings to ensure correct translation between IdP and SP.

Encrypt and sign authentication tokens to prevent unauthorized modification of claims.

Audit claims transformations to detect anomalies in identity attribute processing.

Limit exposure of sensitive attributes, restricting claims to only those required by the SP.

Testing and validation are critical before deploying attribute mapping and claims transformation in production environments. Administrators should use identity debugging tools, such as jwt.io, SAML Tracer, or OpenID Connect Debugger, to inspect authentication tokens and verify that claims are correctly transformed. Conducting integration tests with service providers ensures that attributes are mapped accurately and that authentication flows work as expected.

In federated identity systems, attribute mapping and claims transformation play a crucial role in enabling seamless authentication, enforcing security policies, and ensuring interoperability between identity providers and service providers. By implementing proper attribute translation, applying security controls, and leveraging automation tools, organizations can enhance identity federation while maintaining compliance and access governance.

Identity Governance and Compliance in Federated Identity

Identity governance and compliance are essential components of federated identity management, ensuring that user access is controlled, monitored, and aligned with regulatory requirements. In a federated identity environment, where authentication and authorization are managed across multiple organizations or domains, maintaining strong governance policies is critical to preventing unauthorized access, ensuring data privacy, and demonstrating compliance with industry standards.

Identity governance involves establishing policies, procedures, and controls to manage the lifecycle of user identities, access permissions, and authentication mechanisms. It ensures that users have the appropriate level of access to systems and applications while preventing excessive privileges, orphaned accounts, and access creep. Effective governance minimizes security risks and helps organizations comply with regulations such as GDPR, HIPAA, SOX, and PCI DSS, which mandate strict identity and access controls.

Federated identity governance requires a centralized framework that enables administrators to enforce consistent access control policies across different service providers (SPs) and identity providers (IdPs). This involves defining role-based access control (RBAC) and attribute-based access control (ABAC) policies to ensure that users only access the resources necessary for their job functions. In an RBAC model, users are assigned roles based on their organizational responsibilities, while ABAC considers additional attributes such as department, geographic location, device type, and authentication method to enforce dynamic access decisions.

A key component of identity governance is identity lifecycle management, which governs how user identities are created, modified, and deactivated. When a new user joins an organization, their identity must be provisioned across federated systems, granting them appropriate access based on their role. Similarly, when an employee changes departments or job functions, their access permissions must be updated to reflect their new responsibilities. When users leave the organization, deprovisioning must occur immediately to prevent unauthorized access. Automating these processes using System for Cross-domain Identity Management (SCIM) protocols helps ensure consistency and reduces manual errors.

Access certification and periodic access reviews are critical for maintaining compliance in federated identity environments. Organizations must regularly review user access permissions to ensure that they remain appropriate. Access certifications involve managers or system owners reviewing user entitlements to determine whether they should be maintained, modified, or revoked. This process helps identify inactive accounts, unnecessary privileges, and policy violations that could pose security risks. Automated identity governance solutions provide tools for scheduling and tracking access reviews, ensuring compliance with audit requirements.

Federated identity governance also includes privileged access management (PAM), which controls access to administrative accounts and sensitive resources. Privileged accounts, such as system administrators, database administrators, and security personnel, have elevated access rights that must be carefully managed. In a federated environment, organizations must enforce strict authentication policies, session monitoring, and just-in-time (JIT) access provisioning to reduce the risk of privilege escalation attacks. Implementing multi-factor authentication (MFA) for privileged users adds an additional layer of security.

Identity auditing and logging play a crucial role in governance and compliance. Organizations must maintain detailed logs of authentication and authorization events, tracking who accessed which systems, from where, and at what time. These logs provide forensic evidence in case of security incidents and help demonstrate compliance with regulatory frameworks. Logs should be integrated with Security Information and Event Management (SIEM) systems to enable real-time monitoring, anomaly detection, and automated threat response.

Compliance with regulatory requirements is a major driver for federated identity governance. Different industries and regions impose specific identity security and data protection requirements that organizations must follow:

GDPR (General Data Protection Regulation) mandates strict controls over user identity data, requiring organizations to implement data minimization, consent management, and access transparency. Federated identity systems must ensure that personal data shared between IdPs and SPs is encrypted, limited to necessary attributes, and compliant with user consent preferences.

HIPAA (Health Insurance Portability and Accountability Act) enforces strong identity controls for healthcare organizations, requiring secure authentication, role-based access policies, and detailed audit logging to protect sensitive health information.

SOX (Sarbanes-Oxley Act) requires financial institutions to enforce strict access control measures, periodic access reviews, and real-time monitoring of authentication events.

PCI DSS (Payment Card Industry Data Security Standard) requires organizations handling payment transactions to protect user identities, enforce multi-factor authentication, and restrict privileged access to financial systems.

Ensuring compliance in federated identity environments involves implementing policy-based access control, which dynamically enforces security policies based on real-time risk assessments. Organizations use risk-based authentication (RBA) to evaluate user behavior, geographic location, IP reputation, and device health before granting access. If an authentication attempt appears suspicious, additional security measures, such as step-up authentication or session risk scoring, can be applied to prevent unauthorized access.

Federated identity governance also extends to third-party access management, ensuring that external vendors, partners, and contractors have appropriate access controls. Organizations must establish vendor access policies, defining what resources external users can access and enforcing time-limited access privileges. Implementing federation with external identity providers (such as business partners' IdPs) ensures that third-party users authenticate through trusted identity sources while maintaining auditability and access control enforcement.

To enhance governance, many organizations implement identity analytics and artificial intelligence (AI)-driven identity management. Machine learning algorithms analyze authentication patterns, detect anomalies, and recommend automated access adjustments. Identity analytics help organizations identify excessive permissions, dormant accounts, and high-risk user behaviors, improving security posture while reducing administrative workload.

Federated identity governance frameworks must also include incident response planning for identity-related security breaches. If an identity provider or service provider is compromised, organizations must have predefined incident response procedures to revoke access, reset authentication credentials, and investigate potential data exposure. Implementing automated access revocation and enforcing identity recovery protocols help mitigate the impact of security incidents.

Organizations deploying federated identity solutions must also consider legal and contractual obligations when sharing authentication data across domains. Identity federation agreements between entities must define data sharing policies, access control responsibilities, security requirements, and compliance enforcement mechanisms. These agreements ensure that all parties adhere to regulatory standards while maintaining interoperability and trust in the federated ecosystem.

Adopting Zero Trust principles further strengthens federated identity governance. Instead of assuming trust based on network location, Zero Trust mandates continuous authentication, real-time access verification, and least privilege enforcement. Organizations integrating Zero Trust Identity and Access Management (IAM) into their federated identity architecture can better prevent lateral movement, detect compromised accounts, and enforce least privilege access at all times.

A well-defined identity governance and compliance strategy in federated identity environments helps organizations manage user identities, enforce security controls, and comply with industry regulations. By integrating automated provisioning, access reviews, privileged access management, auditing, and risk-based authentication, organizations can maintain secure, scalable, and compliant federated identity ecosystems.

Common Security Risks in Federated Identity

Federated identity systems provide seamless authentication across multiple organizations and applications, improving security and user experience by reducing password fatigue and enabling Single Sign-On (SSO). However, they also introduce unique security risks that organizations must mitigate to prevent unauthorized access, data breaches, and identity theft. The security of a federated identity system depends on strong authentication mechanisms, trust relationships between identity providers (IdPs) and service providers (SPs), and secure token handling. Without proper safeguards, attackers can exploit vulnerabilities in authentication protocols, session management, and access control policies.

One of the most critical risks in federated identity is identity provider compromise. Since the IdP serves as the central authority for authentication, a breach at this level can grant attackers access to all connected service providers. If an IdP is compromised, attackers can issue valid authentication tokens, bypassing security measures at the SP level. To mitigate this risk, organizations must implement multi-factor authentication (MFA), strict access controls, and continuous monitoring of authentication requests. Additionally, federated identity systems should enforce least privilege access for IdP administrators and use hardware security modules (HSMs) for cryptographic key management.

Man-in-the-middle (MITM) attacks pose another significant threat in federated authentication flows. If an attacker intercepts authentication requests or responses between an IdP and an SP, they may attempt to steal session tokens or manipulate authentication assertions. This risk is particularly high if authentication messages are not properly encrypted. Organizations must enforce end-to-end encryption using TLS (Transport Layer Security) with strong cipher suites and validate certificate authenticity to prevent MITM attacks.

Token theft and replay attacks are common risks in federated identity systems. Attackers who obtain valid authentication tokens can reuse them to impersonate users. If a token is not properly protected, it may be stolen through session hijacking, cross-site scripting (XSS), or token leakage in logs or URLs. To mitigate token theft, organizations should enforce short token lifetimes, use refresh tokens securely, and bind tokens to specific user sessions and devices. Additionally, token signing and encryption should be enabled to prevent unauthorized modification or reuse.

Improper session management can lead to session fixation and session hijacking attacks. If a user remains authenticated for an extended period, an attacker who gains access to their session can perform unauthorized actions. To reduce this risk, federated identity systems should enforce automatic session expiration, session revocation mechanisms, and re-authentication for sensitive operations. Using Secure HTTP-only cookies instead of storing tokens in browser local storage can also protect against XSS attacks.

Another critical risk in federated identity is insecure trust relationships between IdPs and SPs. If an SP incorrectly validates authentication assertions or fails to verify signatures, it may accept forged tokens, allowing attackers to gain unauthorized access. Misconfigured trust relationships can also enable authentication assertion injection, where an attacker crafts a fake assertion to bypass authentication. Organizations must ensure that SPs properly validate SAML assertions, OpenID Connect ID tokens, and OAuth access tokens using public key cryptography. Additionally, IdPs and SPs should regularly update federation metadata and enforce certificate rotation to prevent expired or compromised keys from being exploited.

Privilege escalation attacks occur when an attacker manipulates identity attributes or role claims in authentication tokens to gain higher privileges than intended. If an SP does not properly enforce role-based access control (RBAC) or validate identity attributes received from the IdP, users may be granted excessive permissions. To prevent privilege escalation, federated identity systems should implement attribute validation, claims transformation rules, and role-mapping policies that enforce strict access control based on user identity and organizational policies.

Cross-domain identity federation risks arise when organizations integrate multiple identity providers, including third-party IdPs. If a federated partner has weak security practices, it can introduce vulnerabilities into the entire authentication ecosystem. Attackers may attempt to exploit weakly secured identity providers to gain access to federated applications. To mitigate this risk, organizations must enforce strict federation agreements, conduct regular security audits of third-party IdPs, and implement conditional access policies that restrict authentication from untrusted identity sources.

Insufficient logging and monitoring can allow attacks to go undetected in federated identity systems. Without proper visibility into authentication events, organizations may fail to detect anomalous login activity, failed authentication attempts, or unusual access patterns. To strengthen security, organizations should integrate federated authentication logs with Security Information and Event Management (SIEM) systems to enable real-time threat detection and incident response. Logs should include details such as authentication timestamps, IP addresses, device information, and authentication method used to help security teams identify potential attacks.

Account linking vulnerabilities in federated identity environments can also introduce security risks. Many organizations allow users to link accounts from different IdPs, such as corporate credentials and social identity providers (e.g., Google, Facebook). If an attacker exploits weak account linking mechanisms, they can hijack legitimate user accounts by linking unauthorized identities. To mitigate this risk, organizations should require strong identity proofing methods, enforce MFA for account linking, and implement verification workflows before allowing identity federation between different providers.

Denial-of-Service (DoS) attacks on identity providers can disrupt authentication services and prevent legitimate users from accessing federated applications. Attackers may attempt to flood an IdP with excessive authentication requests or exploit vulnerabilities in authentication protocols to cause system failures. Organizations should implement rate limiting, load balancing, and automated anomaly detection to defend against authentication-based DoS attacks. Additionally, federated authentication services should have failover mechanisms and backup identity providers to ensure business continuity during service disruptions.

Regulatory and compliance risks in federated identity must also be considered. Many organizations are subject to data protection regulations, such as GDPR, CCPA, and HIPAA, which impose strict requirements on identity data handling, consent management, and access control. Federated identity solutions must ensure that user attributes are shared only when necessary and that authentication logs comply with data retention policies. Organizations should also implement privacy-preserving authentication mechanisms, such as anonymous credentials or minimal disclosure tokens, to limit the exposure of personal information.

Emerging threats such as AI-powered phishing and credential stuffing attacks are also impacting federated identity security. Attackers use machine learning algorithms to craft highly convincing phishing emails, tricking users into revealing their authentication credentials. They also leverage leaked password databases to attempt mass login attempts across federated applications. To mitigate these threats, organizations should enforce passwordless authentication methods, such as biometric authentication, FIDO2 security keys, and risk-based authentication policies that detect unusual login behavior.

Federated identity systems provide many security benefits, but they must be properly configured and continuously monitored to prevent security breaches. By implementing strong authentication policies, securing token exchanges, enforcing access controls, and monitoring authentication activity, organizations can build a resilient federated identity infrastructure that protects against emerging threats.

Protecting Against Man-in-the-Middle (MITM) Attacks in SSO

Man-in-the-Middle (MITM) attacks are a serious threat in Single Sign-On (SSO) implementations, where attackers intercept communication between an identity provider (IdP) and a service provider (SP) to steal authentication tokens, credentials, or sensitive identity information. Since SSO systems rely on authentication assertions and token exchanges to grant access across multiple applications, a successful MITM attack can result in unauthorized access to critical resources. Organizations must implement strong encryption, authentication safeguards, and session security mechanisms to protect against these threats.

One of the most effective ways to prevent MITM attacks in SSO is enforcing end-to-end encryption using Transport Layer Security (TLS). TLS encrypts authentication requests and responses between the user, IdP, and SP, preventing attackers from intercepting and reading sensitive data. Organizations should use TLS 1.2 or higher, disable outdated protocols such as SSL and TLS 1.0, and enforce strict cipher suites that resist cryptographic attacks. Additionally, certificate pinning can be implemented to ensure that the authentication endpoints only communicate with trusted identity providers, preventing attackers from using fraudulent certificates to intercept authentication traffic.

Mutual TLS (mTLS) is an advanced security measure that provides bidirectional authentication between the IdP and SP. Unlike standard TLS, which only verifies the identity of the server, mTLS requires both parties to authenticate using digital certificates. This prevents attackers from impersonating an IdP or SP and ensures that only authorized entities can participate in authentication exchanges. mTLS is particularly useful in high-security environments where organizations must defend against sophisticated MITM attacks targeting federated authentication flows.

Another critical security measure is digital signature validation for authentication assertions. In SAML-based SSO, the IdP signs SAML assertions using its private key, and the SP verifies the signature using the IdP's public key. This ensures that authentication tokens cannot be altered or forged by attackers attempting to inject malicious authentication responses. Similarly, in OpenID Connect and OAuth 2.0, ID tokens and access tokens should be digitally signed using JSON Web Signatures (JWS) to maintain integrity and authenticity. Organizations must configure their service providers to reject unsigned or tampered authentication assertions, reducing the risk of MITM exploits.

Strict hostname verification and domain validation help protect against attackers who attempt to redirect authentication requests to fraudulent servers. Attackers often use techniques such as DNS spoofing or rogue access points to intercept authentication traffic and impersonate an identity provider. To prevent this, organizations should enforce hardcoded authentication endpoints, validate the

Issuer (iss) claim in OpenID Connect ID tokens, and ensure that SAML metadata is correctly configured to only trust authorized IdPs. Additionally, enforcing HTTP Strict Transport Security (HSTS) prevents browsers from making unencrypted HTTP requests that could be intercepted.

OAuth 2.0 Proof Key for Code Exchange (PKCE) is an essential security enhancement for authorization code flow in OAuth-based SSO implementations. PKCE mitigates MITM attacks by requiring the client application to generate a random code verifier when requesting an authorization code. When the client exchanges the authorization code for an access token, it must provide the correct code verifier, ensuring that an attacker cannot intercept and reuse authorization codes. PKCE is particularly important for mobile and single-page applications (SPAs) that cannot securely store client secrets.

Implementing multi-factor authentication (MFA) at the IdP level provides an additional layer of security against MITM attacks. Even if an attacker manages to intercept authentication credentials, they will still need the second authentication factor, such as a hardware token, biometric verification, or a one-time passcode (OTP), to complete the authentication process. Adaptive MFA, which requires additional verification for high-risk login attempts, further strengthens protection by prompting users for extra authentication only when suspicious activity is detected.

Session binding and token audience restrictions ensure that authentication tokens are only valid for the intended client and cannot be stolen or reused by an attacker. In OpenID Connect, the aud (audience) claim in the ID token must match the service provider's identifier, preventing attackers from presenting stolen tokens to unauthorized applications. In SAML, recipient validation ensures that authentication assertions are only processed by the designated SP. Binding authentication sessions to specific devices or IP addresses further limits the risk of token hijacking in federated identity environments.

Preventing session fixation and hijacking is another key aspect of protecting against MITM attacks. Attackers can attempt to steal active authentication sessions by injecting session tokens into an authenticated user's browser. To mitigate this risk, organizations should implement same-site cookies, enforce automatic session expiration, and use signed and encrypted session cookies that cannot be manipulated by attackers. Additionally, implementing OAuth token revocation ensures that compromised access tokens can be invalidated if suspicious activity is detected.

Logging and monitoring authentication events help detect potential MITM attacks in real time. Organizations should configure their IdPs and SPs to log failed authentication attempts, token validation errors, and unusual login behaviors. Integrating these logs with Security Information and Event Management (SIEM) systems enables real-time analysis, anomaly detection, and automated incident response. Security teams should actively monitor for signs of MITM attack patterns, such as repeated authentication failures from unknown locations or sudden changes in device fingerprints.

Organizations should also educate users on the risks of MITM attacks and encourage best practices, such as avoiding public Wi-Fi for authentication, verifying URLs before entering credentials, and using VPNs for secure connections. Attackers often exploit unsecured networks to intercept authentication traffic, making user awareness a critical factor in mitigating MITM threats. Security training and awareness campaigns should reinforce the importance of checking for HTTPS in authentication portals, avoiding clicking on suspicious authentication links, and reporting phishing attempts.

Regular penetration testing and security assessments should be conducted to identify and remediate vulnerabilities in federated SSO implementations. Security teams should test for TLS misconfigurations, authentication token leaks, session fixation weaknesses, and replay attack vectors to ensure that authentication flows remain resilient against MITM attacks. Automated security scanners and manual code reviews should be used to detect potential flaws in token validation and encryption mechanisms.

By implementing robust encryption, authentication safeguards, session security controls, and continuous monitoring, organizations can effectively mitigate the risk of MITM attacks in SSO environments. Strengthening security across federated authentication flows, token exchanges, and session management ensures that authentication data remains protected from interception and unauthorized manipulation.

Token Hijacking and Replay Attacks: Prevention Strategies

Token hijacking and replay attacks are significant security threats in identity and access management systems, particularly in federated identity environments where authentication relies on tokens rather than direct credential verification. These attacks occur when an adversary captures a valid authentication token and reuses it to impersonate a legitimate user, gaining unauthorized access to protected resources. Attackers can exploit insecure transmission channels, misconfigured authentication flows, or session management vulnerabilities to execute these attacks. Organizations must implement strong encryption, token validation mechanisms, and session security measures to protect against token hijacking and replay attacks.

Token hijacking occurs when an attacker steals a user's authentication token, such as a JSON Web Token (JWT), SAML assertion, or OAuth access token, and uses it to gain access to an application or service. This can happen through man-in-the-middle (MITM) attacks, cross-site scripting (XSS), session fixation, or local storage compromise in browser-based applications. Once an attacker possesses a valid token, they can bypass authentication mechanisms and operate within the system as the legitimate user.

Replay attacks occur when a previously captured authentication token or session is replayed to gain unauthorized access. Since authentication tokens are often valid for a certain duration, an attacker can intercept a token, store it, and reuse it later before it expires. This attack is particularly dangerous in federated SSO environments, where a stolen token can grant access to multiple systems at once.

Transport Layer Security (TLS) enforcement is the first and most crucial defense against token hijacking. Organizations must enforce TLS 1.2 or higher to encrypt token transmission between clients, identity providers (IdPs), and service providers (SPs). Disabling outdated protocols such as SSL and TLS 1.0/1.1 and enforcing HSTS (HTTP Strict Transport Security) prevents attackers from forcing downgrades to insecure connections. TLS ensures that authentication tokens are not exposed in plaintext over the network, reducing the risk of interception.

Token expiration policies play a key role in limiting the window of opportunity for attackers. Access tokens, ID tokens, and SAML assertions should have short lifetimes to reduce the risk of reuse. OAuth 2.0 tokens typically expire within minutes, requiring applications to obtain fresh tokens periodically. For long-lived authentication sessions, refresh tokens should be used with rotation mechanisms, ensuring that compromised tokens become invalid as soon as they are used. Organizations should configure refresh token policies that enforce session revalidation, preventing attackers from persisting stolen tokens indefinitely.

Binding tokens to specific client devices strengthens security by ensuring that tokens are valid only when used from the device that originally requested them. This is particularly effective in mobile authentication and web-based SSO implementations. Techniques such as OAuth 2.0 token binding and client certificate authentication link authentication tokens to specific hardware or cryptographic keys, making it difficult for attackers to reuse stolen tokens on a different device.

To prevent replay attacks, organizations must implement nonce and timestamp validation in authentication tokens. A nonce (number used once) is a randomly generated value included in authentication requests to prevent attackers from replaying previously used requests. Identity providers must enforce nonce validation in OpenID Connect ID tokens and SAML assertions, rejecting authentication attempts that reuse old nonces. Similarly, timestamp validation ensures that tokens are only valid within a specified time frame. If a token's timestamp is outside the expected window, it is rejected as a potential replay attempt.

OAuth 2.0 Proof Key for Code Exchange (PKCE) is another essential measure for preventing token interception in authorization code flow. PKCE requires the client application to generate a random code verifier and code challenge when requesting an authorization code. When exchanging the code for an access token, the client must provide the correct code verifier, ensuring that an attacker who intercepts the authorization code cannot reuse it without knowing the original challenge. PKCE is particularly important for public clients such as mobile apps and single-page applications (SPAs), where storing secrets securely is difficult.

Audience restrictions and token scoping prevent stolen tokens from being used outside their intended context. The aud (audience) claim in OpenID Connect ID tokens specifies which service provider should accept the token. If an attacker attempts to present the token to an unauthorized service, it will be rejected. Similarly, OAuth 2.0 access tokens should be issued with scopes that limit their access rights, ensuring that even if a token is stolen, it cannot be used to perform actions beyond its original purpose.

Session management and revocation mechanisms are critical for mitigating token hijacking. Organizations must implement OAuth token revocation endpoints, allowing users and administrators to revoke compromised tokens immediately. Implementing Single Logout (SLO) in SAML-based SSO ensures that when a user logs out from one federated service, their session is invalidated across all connected applications. Additionally, idle session timeouts should be enforced to automatically log out users after a period of inactivity, reducing the risk of session hijacking.

Storing tokens securely is essential to prevent theft from local storage or browser memory. Web applications should avoid storing OAuth access tokens and ID tokens in local storage or session storage, as these locations are vulnerable to XSS attacks. Instead, tokens should be stored in HTTP-only, Secure cookies, which are inaccessible to JavaScript and protected from client-side scripting attacks.

Monitoring and anomaly detection help identify suspicious token activity before an attacker can exploit a stolen token. Organizations should log authentication events, including failed login attempts, token refresh attempts, and access token usage patterns. Security teams can analyze logs for anomalies, such as tokens being used from multiple geographic locations within a short time frame, indicating a possible hijacking attempt. Integrating these logs with Security Information and Event Management (SIEM) systems enables real-time threat detection and automated incident response.

Multi-factor authentication (MFA) significantly reduces the risk of token hijacking by requiring additional verification beyond the authentication token. Even if an attacker obtains a valid authentication token, they would still need to provide a second factor, such as a one-time passcode (OTP), biometric authentication, or a security key, to gain access. Organizations should enforce adaptive MFA policies, triggering additional authentication for high-risk scenarios such as logins from new devices, unusual locations, or abnormal access patterns.

Regular penetration testing and security audits help identify vulnerabilities in token handling and authentication flows. Security teams should conduct tests for token leakage, replay attack vectors, session fixation risks, and MITM attack scenarios. Automated security scanners and manual code reviews should be used to ensure that token validation mechanisms are correctly implemented and resistant to common attack patterns.

By implementing secure token handling practices, strong authentication policies, and real-time monitoring, organizations can effectively protect against token hijacking and replay attacks, ensuring the integrity and security of their federated identity environments.

Securing Identity Federation with Certificate Management

Certificate management is a crucial component of securing identity federation, ensuring the integrity, confidentiality, and authenticity of authentication transactions between identity providers (IdPs) and service providers (SPs). In federated identity environments, authentication tokens, security assertions, and API communications rely on public key infrastructure (PKI) and digital certificates to establish trust and prevent unauthorized access. Proper certificate lifecycle management, including issuance, rotation, revocation, and expiration monitoring, is essential to maintaining a secure and resilient identity federation system.

In federated identity, certificates play a key role in signing authentication assertions and encrypting communications. Identity providers use digital certificates to sign SAML assertions, OpenID Connect (OIDC) ID tokens, and OAuth 2.0 access tokens, ensuring that authentication messages cannot be tampered with by malicious actors. Service providers validate these signatures using the public key provided by the IdP's metadata to verify the authenticity of authentication responses. Without proper certificate validation, an attacker could forge authentication assertions, gaining unauthorized access to protected resources.

Encryption certificates are also used to protect sensitive identity attributes transmitted between IdPs and SPs. When an IdP issues an authentication assertion, it may contain user attributes such as email, roles, or group memberships, which must be securely transmitted to the SP. By encrypting these assertions with the SP's public key, identity federation systems ensure that only the intended recipient can decrypt and process the authentication message. This prevents man-in-the-middle (MITM) attacks and unauthorized interception of identity data.

Certificate lifecycle management is critical to maintaining a secure federated identity infrastructure. Organizations must implement automated certificate issuance, renewal, and expiration tracking to prevent authentication disruptions. Expired or revoked certificates can cause authentication failures, breaking Single Sign-On (SSO) workflows and preventing users from accessing federated applications. By maintaining a centralized certificate authority (CA) or leveraging managed certificate services, organizations can ensure continuous availability and security of authentication certificates.

One of the most common security risks in certificate management is certificate expiration leading to service disruptions. If an IdP or SP fails to update an expiring certificate, authentication requests may be rejected, preventing users from logging into federated applications. To mitigate this risk, organizations should configure certificate expiration alerts, enabling administrators to rotate certificates before they expire. Automated tools such as Let's Encrypt, HashiCorp Vault, and AWS Certificate Manager provide built-in renewal mechanisms that simplify certificate management.

Certificate rotation is another critical security practice. Long-lived certificates pose a risk because if a private key is compromised, attackers can use it to sign fraudulent authentication assertions. Organizations should enforce regular certificate rotation policies, replacing signing and encryption certificates at least annually or more frequently based on security requirements. Rotating certificates ensures that even if a private key is exposed, it remains valid only for a limited period, reducing the risk of misuse.

Certificate revocation is essential for responding to security incidents involving compromised credentials. If an IdP's signing certificate is leaked or suspected to be compromised, it must be revoked immediately to prevent unauthorized authentication assertions from being trusted. Organizations should maintain a certificate revocation list (CRL) or use Online Certificate Status Protocol (OCSP) to verify certificate validity dynamically. Service providers must check certificate revocation status before accepting authentication assertions to ensure they are not relying on compromised credentials.

Trust management between identity federation partners requires strict validation of certificate chains and certificate authorities. When an organization federates with external IdPs, it must validate that the presented certificates are issued by a trusted CA and have not been tampered with. Self-signed certificates introduce security risks, as they lack an independent verification authority. Organizations should mandate that only certificates from trusted CAs be accepted and enforce policies for mutual TLS (mTLS) authentication in federated API integrations.

Transport Layer Security (TLS) certificates are essential for securing identity federation transactions. Federated identity systems rely on TLS to encrypt authentication requests, session tokens, and identity assertions sent over the network. Organizations should enforce TLS 1.2 or higher, disable outdated protocols such as TLS 1.0 and SSL, and use strong cipher suites to protect authentication flows from MITM attacks. Additionally, implementing TLS certificate pinning prevents attackers from using fraudulent certificates to intercept authentication traffic.

Federation metadata contains the public keys used for validating authentication assertions and encrypting identity attributes. IdPs and SPs must ensure that their federation metadata is updated whenever certificates are rotated or renewed. If an IdP updates its signing certificate but does not update the corresponding metadata in the SP, authentication requests may fail due to signature validation errors. Automating federation metadata refresh mechanisms ensures that certificate updates are propagated across all federated entities, preventing authentication disruptions.

Federated identity providers must enforce strict access controls for certificate storage and private key management. Signing and encryption private keys must be stored in a secure, isolated environment, such as a hardware security module (HSM) or a cloud-based key management system (KMS). Storing private keys in plaintext on an application server exposes them to theft, increasing the risk of authentication forgery. Using role-based access control (RBAC) and audit logging for certificate access ensures that only authorized personnel can manage private keys.

Certificate transparency and auditing help organizations detect unauthorized changes to certificate configurations. Implementing certificate monitoring solutions allows security teams to track certificate issuance, expiration, and revocation events across all federated identity components. Logs should be integrated with Security Information and Event Management (SIEM) systems to detect anomalies such as unauthorized certificate issuance, unexpected certificate changes, or failed authentication attempts due to invalid certificates.

Federated identity systems must also consider cross-border compliance requirements when managing certificates. Data protection regulations such as GDPR, HIPAA, and CCPA require organizations to implement strong encryption measures for identity data shared between IdPs and SPs. Ensuring that authentication assertions and tokens are encrypted using compliant cryptographic standards helps organizations meet regulatory requirements while maintaining secure authentication flows.

For organizations adopting zero trust security models, certificate-based authentication enhances access control by replacing traditional credentials with mutual certificate verification. Instead of relying solely on passwords or federated tokens, organizations can require users and devices to authenticate using X.509 certificates, ensuring that only trusted entities access federated applications. Zero trust architectures leverage continuous certificate validation and dynamic policy enforcement to prevent unauthorized access.

Securing identity federation with certificate management requires a combination of automated certificate lifecycle management, strong cryptographic enforcement, and continuous monitoring. By implementing strict certificate validation policies, enforcing encryption for authentication assertions, and regularly rotating signing keys, organizations can maintain a robust federated identity infrastructure that protects against unauthorized access and identity fraud.

Managing Session Security and Token Expiry in SSO

Session security and token expiry are critical components of a secure Single Sign-On (SSO) implementation. In federated identity environments, authentication is typically managed using session cookies, security tokens, or authentication assertions, which allow users to access multiple services without repeatedly entering their credentials. However, improper session management can expose organizations to risks such as session hijacking, replay attacks, and unauthorized access due to token misuse. Effective session security ensures that user authentication remains valid only for the intended duration, while token expiry policies limit the risk of token misuse if compromised.

Session management in SSO involves handling user authentication states across identity providers (IdPs) and service providers (SPs). When a user authenticates through an IdP, the authentication state is typically stored as a session cookie in the user's browser or as an authentication token in the application's backend. The session duration determines how long the user remains authenticated before needing to reauthenticate. A poorly configured session policy can either create frustration for users (due to frequent logouts) or security risks (by allowing excessively long sessions that attackers can exploit).

Token expiry policies define how long authentication tokens remain valid before they need to be refreshed. In OAuth 2.0, OpenID Connect (OIDC), and SAML-based SSO, different types of tokens (access tokens, refresh tokens, and ID tokens) have distinct lifespans. Access tokens are used for API authentication and typically have short expiration times, while refresh tokens allow the client to obtain new access tokens without requiring the user to log in again. ID tokens, which contain user identity information, also have expiration settings to ensure that authentication sessions remain secure.

Short-lived access tokens are an essential security measure to reduce the risk of token misuse. If an access token is compromised, an attacker can use it to gain unauthorized access until it expires. Organizations should set access token expiration times between 5 and 30 minutes, depending on the security sensitivity of the application. Short-lived tokens minimize the window of opportunity for attackers while ensuring a seamless user experience through silent token refresh mechanisms.

Refresh tokens allow users to maintain long-lived authentication sessions without exposing long-duration access tokens. Instead of requiring the user to log in again, the client application can use a refresh token to request a new access token when the old one expires.

However, refresh tokens must be securely managed, as their compromise can lead to persistent unauthorized access. To mitigate this risk, organizations should enforce refresh token rotation, where each new access token is issued with a new refresh token, invalidating the previous one. Additionally, revocation mechanisms should allow administrators to invalidate refresh tokens if they suspect compromise.

Session timeout policies help mitigate the risk of session hijacking by automatically logging users out after a period of inactivity. Idle session timeouts should be adjusted based on user risk levels, with higher-risk users (such as privileged administrators) having shorter session durations than regular users. Many security frameworks recommend idle session timeouts of 15-30 minutes for high-risk applications and 60-120 minutes for general user sessions. Applications should also support active session extension, where users can extend their session securely before timeout by reauthenticating.

Session binding enhances security by ensuring that a session is only valid from the specific device and network from which it was initiated. This prevents session hijacking, where an attacker steals an authentication token and replays it from another location. Techniques for session binding include IP address tracking, device fingerprinting, and cryptographic token binding, which ties an authentication token to a specific client instance. If a session token is presented from an unrecognized device or network, the user should be required to reauthenticate.

Single Logout (SLO) ensures that when a user logs out from one service, they are logged out of all federated services. Without SLO, users may log out from one application while remaining authenticated in others, creating a security risk where an attacker can take advantage of lingering authentication states. SLO is implemented using SAML Logout Requests or OIDC End-Session endpoints, notifying all SPs to terminate the user's session upon logout. Organizations should enforce mandatory session revocation across all linked applications to prevent unauthorized access after logout.

Token revocation mechanisms allow administrators to invalidate authentication tokens before they naturally expire. This is essential for scenarios where a token has been compromised or a user's access has been revoked. In OAuth 2.0, token revocation endpoints enable clients to inform the authorization server that a token should no longer be considered valid. Similarly, SAML assertion revocation can be implemented by maintaining a revocation list or leveraging short-lived assertions that automatically expire.

Secure storage of authentication tokens prevents unauthorized access to session data. Web applications should store tokens in HTTP-only, secure cookies instead of local storage, as local storage is vulnerable to cross-site scripting (XSS) attacks. Secure cookies prevent JavaScript-based attacks from accessing authentication tokens, reducing the risk of token theft. Additionally, same-site cookie policies should be enforced to prevent cross-site request forgery (CSRF) attacks, which attempt to exploit active authentication sessions.

Adaptive authentication and risk-based session policies help dynamically adjust session security based on user behavior. Instead of applying a fixed session timeout, organizations can implement continuous authentication, where a user's behavior, device posture, and geolocation influence session validity. If an authentication session appears to be compromised—such as login attempts from multiple geographic locations within a short time frame—the system can trigger step-up authentication, requiring additional verification before continuing the session.

Logging and monitoring session activity helps detect suspicious behavior that may indicate session hijacking, token theft, or unauthorized token reuse. Organizations should log authentication attempts, token refresh events, and logout activities, integrating them with Security Information and Event Management (SIEM) systems for real-time monitoring. Security teams can configure alerts for anomalous session behaviors, such as repeated refresh token usage from different IP addresses, indicating possible token compromise.

Periodic access reviews and session audits are essential for maintaining compliance and security best practices. Organizations should regularly review active sessions, long-lived tokens, and refresh token usage patterns to ensure that session policies remain aligned with evolving security threats. Automated tools can help detect inactive accounts or forgotten sessions, prompting administrators to revoke unused authentication tokens.

A well-designed session security and token expiry strategy balances security, usability, and compliance. Organizations must implement short-lived access tokens, refresh token rotation, session revocation policies, and continuous monitoring to protect against unauthorized session persistence and token-based attacks. By enforcing secure token storage, dynamic session enforcement, and adaptive authentication mechanisms, federated identity systems can minimize the risks associated with compromised authentication tokens and session hijacking.

Zero Trust and Its Relationship with Federated Identity

Zero Trust is a modern security framework that challenges the traditional assumption of implicit trust within a network. Instead of allowing users or devices to access resources based solely on their location or initial authentication, Zero Trust enforces continuous verification at every access request. This model aligns closely with federated identity, where users authenticate through a central identity provider (IdP) to access multiple services. By integrating Zero Trust principles with federated identity, organizations can enforce dynamic access controls, risk-based authentication, and least-privilege access while reducing reliance on traditional perimeter security.

At its core, Zero Trust operates under the principle of "never trust, always verify." This means that authentication is not a one-time event but a continuous process that evaluates users, devices, applications, and network conditions before granting access. Federated identity solutions, such as SAML, OAuth 2.0, and OpenID Connect (OIDC), already support many of the foundational elements of Zero Trust by centralizing identity management and providing Single Sign-On (SSO) for users across different applications. However, traditional federated identity models often assume that once authentication is completed, a user can access multiple resources without additional verification. Zero Trust enhances this model by introducing adaptive authentication and continuous monitoring.

One of the primary security challenges addressed by Zero Trust in federated identity environments is lateral movement attacks. In traditional authentication models, a compromised user credential grants broad access within an organization, allowing attackers to move between applications and services unnoticed. Zero Trust mitigates this risk by enforcing least-privilege access, ensuring that even authenticated users only have access to resources necessary for their job functions. This approach limits the impact of credential theft and prevents unauthorized privilege escalation.

Multi-factor authentication (MFA) and risk-based authentication play a crucial role in integrating Zero Trust with federated identity. While federated identity simplifies user authentication by allowing a single credential set to be used across multiple applications, it also creates a single point of failure if credentials are compromised. By enforcing MFA at the identity provider level, organizations can add an extra layer of security, requiring users to verify their identity using additional factors such as biometric authentication, security keys, or one-time passcodes (OTP).

Risk-based authentication further enhances security by dynamically adjusting authentication requirements based on real-time risk analysis. Factors such as device reputation, geolocation, login behavior, and historical access patterns help determine whether a login attempt is legitimate. If a user logs in from an unfamiliar device or an unusual geographic location, the system can enforce step-up authentication before granting access. This adaptive approach aligns with Zero Trust's emphasis on continuous verification and conditional access.

Micro-segmentation is another key Zero Trust principle that complements federated identity. Instead of granting broad access to all authenticated users, Zero Trust divides network resources into smaller segments and applies strict access controls to each segment. Federated identity supports this model by enabling attribute-based access control (ABAC) and role-based access control (RBAC), where access decisions are based on user attributes, roles, and security policies. This ensures that even if an attacker gains access through compromised credentials, they cannot move freely within the environment.

Zero Trust also addresses the device security challenge in federated identity. In traditional federated authentication, the focus is primarily on verifying who the user is, rather than what device they are using. However, Zero Trust extends authentication policies to include device trust, ensuring that only compliant and secure devices can access protected resources. Identity providers can integrate with endpoint detection and response (EDR) solutions to verify device health, ensuring that access requests come from trusted, up-to-date, and uncompromised endpoints.

Session management and continuous authentication are critical for implementing Zero Trust within federated identity frameworks. Traditional authentication sessions in federated identity systems are often long-lived, meaning that once a user logs in, they maintain access without additional verification for extended periods. Zero Trust introduces session expiration policies and real-time risk assessment, requiring users to reauthenticate periodically or validate access requests dynamically based on changes in risk factors.

Zero Trust architecture also enhances security in cloud and hybrid environments, where federated identity plays a major role in providing seamless authentication across multiple platforms. Cloud applications, third-party services, and on-premises resources all need to be secured under a unified access control model. By integrating Zero Trust principles with federated identity, organizations can enforce consistent security policies across all environments, regardless of where an application is hosted.

Logging and monitoring are essential for maintaining Zero Trust security within federated identity environments. Organizations must continuously track authentication events, user access patterns, and anomalous behavior to detect potential threats. Integrating identity and access logs with Security Information and Event Management (SIEM) systems enables real-time threat detection and automated response mechanisms. Security teams can configure alerts for failed authentication attempts, unauthorized access attempts, and abnormal session behaviors, helping to mitigate insider threats and external attacks.

Another key consideration in applying Zero Trust to federated identity is third-party identity federation risks. Many organizations extend their federated identity framework to include contractors, partners, and external vendors, allowing them to authenticate using their own identity providers. While this improves business-to-business (B2B) collaboration, it also introduces security risks if an external IdP has weaker security controls. Zero Trust mitigates this risk by enforcing conditional access policies, where federated users must meet strict authentication requirements, undergo additional security checks, and operate within predefined access scopes.

Zero Trust also strengthens privileged access management (PAM) in federated identity environments. Administrative and privileged accounts are frequent targets for attackers because they provide elevated access to critical resources. By enforcing Just-in-Time (JIT) privileged access and session monitoring for privileged users, organizations can reduce the risk of privilege escalation attacks. Instead of granting persistent administrative access, Zero Trust policies require users to request elevated permissions only when needed, with approval workflows and additional security checks before access is granted.

For organizations adopting passwordless authentication, Zero Trust and federated identity work together to enhance security and user experience. Traditional passwords remain a weak point in identity security, often leading to credential theft and phishing attacks. Zero Trust frameworks encourage the adoption of FIDO2-based authentication, biometric authentication, and certificate-based authentication, eliminating passwords while ensuring strong, phishing-resistant authentication mechanisms.

Zero Trust is not a replacement for federated identity but rather an evolution that strengthens its security foundation. By combining centralized identity management with continuous authentication, conditional access, and real-time monitoring, organizations can create a more secure authentication framework that minimizes attack surfaces and protects against identity-based threats.

Federation in Multi-Cloud and Hybrid Cloud Environments

Federated identity is a critical component in multi-cloud and hybrid cloud environments, enabling seamless authentication across different cloud platforms and on-premises infrastructures. As organizations increasingly adopt multi-cloud strategies, using services from multiple cloud providers such as AWS, Microsoft Azure, Google Cloud, and Oracle Cloud, the challenge of managing authentication and authorization across disparate systems grows. Federation provides a standardized way to authenticate users and grant access without requiring separate credentials for each environment. In hybrid cloud architectures, where enterprises maintain both on-premises infrastructure and cloud services, identity federation ensures a unified authentication experience, reducing security risks while simplifying user access management.

One of the main drivers for federation in multi-cloud environments is the need for a consistent authentication model across cloud platforms. Without federation, organizations must manage multiple identity silos, leading to increased complexity, security risks, and compliance challenges. Federation allows users to authenticate once with a central identity provider (IdP) and access applications and services hosted on different cloud platforms without re-entering credentials. This is achieved using identity federation protocols such as Security Assertion Markup Language (SAML), OpenID Connect (OIDC), and OAuth 2.0, which enable trust relationships between identity providers and service providers (SPs).

In a hybrid cloud environment, where organizations integrate on-premises Active Directory (AD) or LDAP directories with cloud-based services, identity federation ensures that employees can use their corporate credentials to authenticate across both on-prem and cloud resources. Solutions such as Microsoft Entra ID (formerly Azure AD) Connect, AWS IAM Identity Center, and Google Workspace

Federation enable seamless integration between enterprise directories and cloud identity providers. These solutions synchronize user identities and enforce authentication policies across environments, ensuring consistency in access control.

Single Sign-On (SSO) is a key benefit of identity federation in multi-cloud and hybrid cloud environments. Instead of requiring users to maintain multiple credentials for different cloud services, SSO allows them to log in once and gain access to all federated applications. This enhances security by reducing password reuse and phishing risks while improving the user experience. In a multi-cloud setting, SSO is typically implemented using federation bridges, where a central IdP (such as Okta, Ping Identity, or Microsoft Entra ID) acts as the authentication authority, verifying user credentials and issuing authentication assertions that are accepted by cloud providers.

Security in multi-cloud federation is a significant concern, as federated authentication expands the attack surface across multiple cloud environments. Organizations must enforce strong authentication policies, such as multi-factor authentication (MFA) and risk-based authentication, to prevent unauthorized access. Many cloud providers support adaptive authentication, where authentication requirements dynamically adjust based on risk factors such as geolocation, device security posture, and login behavior. By integrating zero trust principles, organizations can apply continuous authentication and least-privilege access controls to federated identities, reducing the risk of credential compromise.

Another challenge in multi-cloud federation is managing identity synchronization and lifecycle management across multiple cloud platforms. Users may have different roles, permissions, and access policies depending on the cloud services they interact with. To address this, organizations leverage System for Cross-domain Identity Management (SCIM), an open standard that automates user provisioning and deprovisioning across identity systems. SCIM ensures that user attributes remain consistent across cloud platforms and that deprovisioned users lose access immediately, reducing the risk of orphaned accounts.

Inter-cloud federation, where different cloud providers federate identities with one another, is becoming increasingly important in multi-cloud deployments. Many enterprises operate workloads across AWS, Azure, and Google Cloud, requiring seamless authentication between these platforms. Some cloud providers offer native identity federation features, such as AWS IAM Identity Center (formerly AWS SSO) federation with Entra ID or Google Cloud federated login with SAML-based IdPs. These integrations enable enterprises to centralize identity management while extending authentication capabilities to cloud-native applications and services.

Federation also plays a key role in securing hybrid cloud workloads, where applications and services span on-premises and cloud environments. Many organizations rely on hybrid identity solutions, such as Active Directory Federation Services (AD FS) and Azure AD Federation, to bridge authentication between on-prem and cloud applications. This allows enterprises to extend Kerberos-based authentication and group policy enforcement to cloud resources, ensuring compliance with existing security policies. Hybrid federation also enables secure VPN and remote access solutions, allowing employees and contractors to authenticate securely regardless of their location.

In business-to-business (B2B) federation, organizations establish trust relationships with partner companies, vendors, and external service providers to enable secure cross-company authentication. Instead of creating separate user accounts for external users, federation allows partner organizations to authenticate using their own identity providers. Cloud-based solutions such as Microsoft Entra B2B, AWS Cognito, and Google Cloud Identity Federation facilitate secure authentication between organizations, improving collaboration while reducing administrative overhead.

Multi-cloud security challenges in federated identity include token management, session security, and API access control. Cloud environments rely on OAuth 2.0 access tokens and JSON Web Tokens (JWTs) for authentication to APIs and microservices. Proper token expiration policies, audience restrictions, and token revocation mechanisms must be enforced to prevent token hijacking and replay attacks. Cloud providers offer managed token security services, such as

AWS Security Token Service (STS) and Google Cloud IAM access policies, which provide short-lived, dynamically scoped tokens that minimize the risk of misuse.

Federation also enables compliance and auditability in multi-cloud and hybrid cloud environments. Organizations subject to regulatory frameworks such as GDPR, HIPAA, and SOC 2 must enforce identity governance policies across all federated services. Identity logging and monitoring, integrated with Security Information and Event Management (SIEM) systems, allows enterprises to track authentication events, detect anomalies, and generate audit reports. Many cloud platforms provide federated identity logging features, such as AWS CloudTrail, Azure Monitor, and Google Cloud Audit Logs, which capture authentication and access events for compliance reporting.

Federated identity resilience and disaster recovery are important considerations in multi-cloud strategies. If an identity provider experiences downtime, authentication to all federated services could be impacted. To mitigate this risk, organizations should implement redundant IdPs, failover authentication mechanisms, and backup federation configurations. Some enterprises deploy multiple federated identity providers, using Azure AD as a primary IdP and Okta as a secondary failover, ensuring business continuity in case of outages.

Organizations planning to implement federated identity in multi-cloud or hybrid environments must carefully design trust relationships, enforce security best practices, and ensure interoperability between identity providers and cloud platforms. By leveraging SSO, MFA, identity synchronization, and zero trust security models, enterprises can achieve a secure, scalable, and seamless authentication experience across their cloud ecosystem.

Identity Federation in Government and Healthcare Sectors

Identity federation plays a crucial role in the government and healthcare sectors, where secure, seamless, and privacy-compliant authentication is necessary for accessing sensitive systems and data. These sectors manage vast amounts of personally identifiable information (PII) and protected health information (PHI), making security and interoperability key concerns. Federated identity solutions enable secure cross-agency authentication, patient data access, and intergovernmental collaboration, while ensuring compliance with regulatory frameworks such as GDPR, HIPAA, and NIST security standards.

Governments operate complex identity ecosystems that require secure authentication across multiple agencies, departments, and partner organizations. Traditionally, each agency maintained separate identity silos, requiring users to maintain multiple credentials for different government services. Identity federation eliminates this redundancy by allowing users to authenticate once through a trusted identity provider (IdP) and gain access to multiple government applications and services. This improves user experience, security, and administrative efficiency, reducing the risk of credential misuse and password fatigue.

National identity programs are a common use case for federated identity in government. Many countries implement centralized identity systems that serve as trusted IdPs for citizen authentication across government services. Examples include eIDAS in the European Union, Aadhaar in India, and Gov.uk Verify in the United Kingdom. These systems enable federated authentication for tax services, social security benefits, healthcare records, and e-government portals, reducing reliance on password-based authentication and enabling stronger security mechanisms such as smartcards, biometrics, and multi-factor authentication (MFA).

Identity federation also supports business-to-government (B2G) authentication, where private sector organizations authenticate with government services using their corporate identity providers. This is particularly relevant in regulatory compliance scenarios, where businesses need to access government portals for reporting, licensing, and tax filing. By integrating federated authentication with enterprise identity systems such as Microsoft Entra ID (formerly Azure AD), Okta, or Ping Identity, governments can enable secure and scalable third-party access while enforcing strong authentication policies.

In the healthcare sector, federated identity is essential for enabling secure patient data access, provider collaboration, and compliance with privacy regulations. Healthcare organizations manage sensitive patient information, which must be securely shared across hospitals, clinics, insurers, and research institutions. Identity federation allows doctors, nurses, and healthcare administrators to authenticate once and access electronic health records (EHRs), telemedicine platforms, and prescription systems without needing separate logins for each service.

Interoperability between healthcare providers is a major challenge in federated identity management. Many healthcare organizations use different identity systems and authentication standards, leading to fragmentation and security risks. Federated identity helps unify authentication by using standards such as SAML, OpenID Connect (OIDC), and OAuth 2.0, ensuring that users can securely authenticate across different healthcare networks. Initiatives such as Fast Healthcare Interoperability Resources (FHIR) and SMART on FHIR promote secure identity federation in health IT systems, allowing seamless patient data exchange while maintaining strict access controls.

Multi-factor authentication (MFA) and adaptive authentication play a crucial role in securing healthcare identity federation. Given the high risk of medical identity theft, phishing attacks, and unauthorized data access, healthcare organizations must enforce strong authentication policies for both internal users (doctors, nurses, administrators) and external users (patients, insurance providers). Many healthcare IdPs implement risk-based authentication, where login attempts from unfamiliar locations, devices, or networks trigger additional authentication steps, such as one-time passcodes (OTPs) or biometric verification.

Patient authentication is another critical aspect of identity federation in healthcare. Patients need secure access to personal health records, appointment scheduling, and insurance claims, often through web portals or mobile applications. Federated identity enables patients to authenticate using trusted identity providers, such as national health ID systems, insurance provider logins, or commercial authentication providers like Google and Apple ID. This simplifies authentication while maintaining strict privacy controls over patient data sharing.

Telemedicine and remote healthcare services have accelerated the adoption of federated identity in healthcare. With the rise of virtual consultations, remote diagnostics, and digital prescriptions, healthcare providers must ensure that only authorized practitioners and patients can access sensitive medical data. Federated authentication enables secure identity verification for telehealth platforms, reducing the risk of fraudulent access, identity spoofing, and patient data leaks. Many telehealth services integrate with national identity systems or federated healthcare networks, ensuring that authentication complies with regulatory requirements.

Identity governance and compliance are critical for federated identity in both government and healthcare sectors. These industries operate under strict regulatory frameworks, such as HIPAA (Health Insurance Portability and Accountability Act) in the U.S., GDPR (General Data Protection Regulation) in Europe, and NIST 800-63 identity guidelines for U.S. federal agencies. Federated identity solutions must support fine-grained access controls, audit logging, and data protection policies to comply with these regulations.

Role-based access control (RBAC) and attribute-based access control (ABAC) are commonly used in federated identity for government and healthcare. RBAC ensures that users can only access data and systems based on their job functions, while ABAC applies dynamic access policies based on attributes such as device type, location, risk score, and authentication strength. For example, a doctor may have access to patient records within their hospital network, but not external hospital records unless explicitly authorized.

Cross-agency and cross-border identity federation are additional challenges in government and healthcare identity management.

Governments frequently collaborate on international law enforcement, border security, and intelligence sharing, requiring secure authentication across different national identity systems. Similarly, healthcare providers must enable cross-border patient record access, ensuring that doctors in one country can securely retrieve medical history from another country's healthcare system. Standards such as eIDAS (electronic Identification, Authentication, and Trust Services) in the EU facilitate secure cross-border identity federation, ensuring that users can authenticate using their home country's identity provider while complying with local privacy laws.

Security risks in federated identity for government and healthcare include identity spoofing, insider threats, and credential-based attacks. Governments and healthcare providers must implement strict authentication monitoring, anomaly detection, and session security controls to prevent unauthorized access. Federated identity logging and analytics, integrated with Security Information and Event Management (SIEM) systems, help detect suspicious login behaviors, failed authentication attempts, and unauthorized role escalations.

Federation with cloud-based identity providers is becoming increasingly common in government and healthcare digital transformation initiatives. Many agencies and hospitals migrate applications to cloud environments, requiring secure authentication with cloud identity providers such as Microsoft Entra ID, AWS IAM, and Google Cloud Identity. Hybrid identity federation ensures that users can seamlessly authenticate across legacy on-premises applications and modern cloud services, maintaining security and compliance throughout the migration process.

A well-implemented federated identity framework in government and healthcare sectors enhances security, interoperability, and user convenience, allowing trusted authentication across multiple agencies, organizations, and international borders. By leveraging strong authentication mechanisms, adaptive access policies, and continuous identity monitoring, federated identity systems help protect citizen and patient data while enabling efficient, secure, and compliant digital services.

Role-Based Access Control (RBAC) and Attribute-Based Access Control (ABAC)

Role-Based Access Control (RBAC) and Attribute-Based Access Control (ABAC) are two of the most widely used access control models in identity and access management (IAM). These models define how users are granted access to systems, applications, and data based on predefined rules. While both approaches serve the purpose of enforcing security policies, they differ in how they assign permissions and determine access rights. RBAC relies on user roles, while ABAC incorporates dynamic attributes and contextual factors to make access control decisions. Understanding these models is essential for organizations implementing federated identity, Single Sign-On (SSO), and identity governance frameworks.

RBAC is a structured approach to access control where users are assigned roles, and each role is associated with specific permissions. This model is widely used in enterprise environments to simplify user access management and security administration. Roles are typically defined based on job functions, departments, or organizational responsibilities, ensuring that users only have access to resources necessary for their duties.

In an RBAC system, permissions are not assigned directly to individual users but rather to roles, which are then assigned to users. For example:

A Finance Manager role might have access to financial records, budget reports, and accounting software.

A Human Resources Administrator role might be able to access employee records, payroll systems, and benefits portals.

An IT Support Technician role might have privileges to reset passwords, manage user accounts, and troubleshoot system issues.

RBAC helps organizations implement the principle of least privilege (PoLP) by ensuring that users do not receive more permissions than necessary for their job function. This reduces the risk of insider threats, accidental data leaks, and unauthorized privilege escalation.

One of the main advantages of RBAC is its simplicity and scalability. Organizations can define a hierarchical structure where higher roles inherit permissions from lower roles. For example, a Senior Engineer might inherit all the permissions of a Regular Engineer but have additional privileges for approving technical changes. This model is particularly beneficial in large organizations where managing individual user permissions manually would be complex and error-prone.

However, RBAC has limitations, particularly in dynamic or highly regulated environments. It lacks flexibility when access decisions depend on contextual factors such as location, device type, time of access, or security posture. For example, an RBAC policy might allow a Sales Representative to access a customer database, but it cannot enforce restrictions based on whether the user is logging in from an untrusted network or outside working hours. This is where ABAC becomes a more powerful alternative.

ABAC extends RBAC by incorporating real-time attributes and dynamic policies into access control decisions. Instead of relying solely on static roles, ABAC evaluates user attributes, environmental conditions, and resource properties before granting access. Attributes can include user identity attributes (such as department, job title, or security clearance), device information, location, authentication method, and risk scores.

For example, an ABAC policy could enforce the following conditions:

A Doctor can access patient records only if they are within the hospital's network and using an authorized device.

A Remote Employee can access sensitive financial data only if they authenticate using multi-factor authentication (MFA) and their device meets security compliance requirements.

A Cloud Administrator can modify cloud infrastructure settings only if they log in from a corporate-issued laptop and during business hours.

ABAC provides granular access control, making it suitable for highly regulated industries such as healthcare, finance, and government.

Organizations that must comply with regulations such as HIPAA, GDPR, and SOC 2 benefit from ABAC's ability to enforce fine-grained access policies that go beyond role-based permissions.

One of the major advantages of ABAC is its adaptability to changing business needs. Unlike RBAC, where permissions must be manually adjusted when a user's role changes, ABAC dynamically evaluates attributes in real-time to determine whether access should be granted or denied. This reduces the need for manual role adjustments and enhances security by automatically enforcing access restrictions based on context.

Despite its advantages, ABAC has higher implementation complexity compared to RBAC. It requires organizations to define attribute taxonomies, policy enforcement mechanisms, and real-time attribute evaluation engines. Additionally, maintaining attribute consistency across multiple identity providers (IdPs) and service providers (SPs) in a federated identity system can be challenging.

Many organizations adopt a hybrid approach, combining RBAC and ABAC to leverage the benefits of both models. In this approach, RBAC defines baseline access permissions, while ABAC introduces contextual controls to refine access decisions. For example:

A user's role (RBAC) determines their general access to applications.

ABAC policies further restrict access based on conditions such as IP address, device security posture, or risk score.

Hybrid RBAC-ABAC implementations are widely used in Zero Trust security architectures, where access is continuously verified based on real-time conditions rather than being granted indefinitely.

Organizations implementing federated identity solutions, such as SAML-based SSO, OAuth 2.0 authorization, or OpenID Connect authentication, must ensure that RBAC and ABAC policies are consistently enforced across all identity providers and service providers. This requires integration with identity governance platforms, security information and event management (SIEM) tools, and adaptive access controls.

In cloud environments, RBAC and ABAC are essential for securing cloud workloads and API access. Cloud providers such as AWS, Microsoft Azure, and Google Cloud offer role-based access control models for managing infrastructure access, while ABAC can be implemented using cloud-native security policies that restrict access based on device security posture, geolocation, and behavioral analytics.

Ultimately, the choice between RBAC and ABAC depends on an organization's security needs, regulatory requirements, and operational complexity. While RBAC provides a structured, easy-to-manage access control model, ABAC enables dynamic, fine-grained access decisions that adapt to changing conditions. A well-implemented access control strategy ensures strong security, compliance, and efficient identity management in both traditional and federated identity environments.

Integrating SSO with Mobile and IoT Devices

The integration of Single Sign-On (SSO) with mobile devices and Internet of Things (IoT) devices presents unique challenges and security considerations. Unlike traditional desktop environments, mobile and IoT ecosystems involve diverse operating systems, device constraints, network variability, and varying security postures. As organizations expand their digital ecosystems, enabling seamless yet secure authentication across smartphones, tablets, wearables, and IoT devices is essential. By leveraging modern authentication protocols such as OAuth 2.0, OpenID Connect (OIDC), and device-bound credentials, organizations can extend SSO capabilities while maintaining strong security controls.

Mobile SSO allows users to authenticate once and access multiple applications without repeatedly entering credentials. Given the rise of enterprise mobility, bring-your-own-device (BYOD) policies, and cloud-based applications, implementing mobile SSO ensures a frictionless user experience while reducing security risks associated with password reuse and phishing attacks. OAuth 2.0 with OpenID Connect is the most common authentication framework for mobile SSO, enabling applications to authenticate users through an identity provider (IdP) while leveraging security tokens for session management.

One of the main challenges of mobile SSO is managing secure authentication across multiple applications on a single device. Unlike web-based SSO, where authentication happens through a centralized browser session, mobile applications often require application-specific authentication workflows. To address this, mobile platforms support shared authentication sessions, where a user logs in once, and subsequent applications retrieve authentication tokens from a secure session store or a centralized identity provider.

For example, Apple's Single Sign-On (SSO) framework allows apps from the same organization to share authentication tokens, reducing redundant login prompts. Similarly, Google Smart Lock for Passwords and Android Account Manager enable persistent authentication across multiple apps. Mobile authentication SDKs from identity providers such as Okta, Autho, and Microsoft Entra ID (formerly Azure AD) provide pre-built mobile SSO solutions that integrate with native authentication flows.

Security considerations for mobile SSO include protecting authentication tokens, mitigating session hijacking risks, and ensuring secure token storage. Since mobile devices are more susceptible to theft, malware, and unauthorized access, authentication tokens should be stored securely using encrypted device storage, hardware-backed keychains, or secure enclaves. In iOS and Android, secure storage APIs such as iOS Keychain and Android Keystore allow apps to store authentication tokens securely, preventing exposure through malware or rogue applications.

Biometric authentication enhances mobile SSO security by enabling passwordless authentication using fingerprint recognition, facial recognition, or device PINs. Many mobile identity providers support FIDO2 and WebAuthn, allowing biometric-based authentication for

SSO without relying on passwords. For example, a user logging into a corporate mobile application can authenticate using Face ID or fingerprint authentication, with the system verifying identity through a secure enclave rather than sending passwords over the network.

IoT devices present additional challenges for SSO integration due to their limited processing power, constrained user interfaces, and lack of traditional authentication inputs. Unlike mobile devices, most IoT devices do not support traditional login mechanisms such as usernames and passwords. Instead, IoT authentication relies on device-bound credentials, certificates, and OAuth 2.0-based device authorization flows.

OAuth 2.0 Device Flow is commonly used for IoT authentication, allowing headless devices (such as smart TVs, IoT sensors, and industrial controllers) to authenticate without a traditional UI. In this model, the IoT device displays a one-time authorization code, and the user completes authentication on a separate device, such as a smartphone or computer. Once authentication is completed, the IoT device receives an OAuth access token, enabling secure communication with cloud services.

For example, a smart home security camera using OAuth 2.0 Device Flow might display an activation code on its screen. The user enters this code on their smartphone, authenticates through an identity provider (e.g., Google, Microsoft, or a corporate IdP), and grants the camera access to their cloud storage. Once authorized, the camera receives an access token and can securely upload footage to the cloud.

Certificate-based authentication is another common approach for IoT SSO, where each device is issued a unique cryptographic certificate instead of a username and password. These certificates allow devices to authenticate against identity providers or cloud platforms securely, reducing the risk of credential-based attacks. Mutual TLS (mTLS) further strengthens IoT security by requiring both the device and server to authenticate each other using certificates.

Federated identity in IoT ecosystems enables organizations to manage authentication across heterogeneous device environments spanning multiple vendors and platforms. Cloud-based identity solutions such as AWS IoT, Microsoft Entra ID (Azure IoT), and Google Cloud Identity-Aware Proxy (IAP) support federated authentication, allowing IoT devices to authenticate against a central identity provider while enforcing role-based or attribute-based access controls.

Session security and token expiration are critical in mobile and IoT SSO implementations. Unlike traditional desktops, mobile and IoT devices frequently change networks, switch between cellular and Wi-Fi connections, or enter sleep states. This variability introduces risks of session persistence and token misuse. Organizations must implement short-lived access tokens with refresh token rotation to ensure that authentication sessions remain valid only when actively used.

For example, a mobile banking app might issue an OAuth access token valid for 15 minutes and require silent token refresh using a refresh token to maintain authentication. If a risk-based policy detects an unusual login attempt or device anomaly, it can trigger step-up authentication, requiring the user to re-enter their password or verify through biometric authentication.

Zero Trust principles in mobile and IoT authentication emphasize continuous validation of user and device identities rather than relying on one-time authentication events. By integrating risk-based authentication, device posture assessment, and adaptive security policies, organizations can enhance mobile and IoT SSO security. For example, an enterprise may require that mobile devices meet compliance policies (e.g., encryption enabled, latest OS updates) before granting access to corporate resources.

Security monitoring and anomaly detection are essential for identifying suspicious authentication behaviors in mobile and IoT environments. Identity providers should log authentication events, including failed login attempts, token refresh requests, and device location changes, feeding this data into Security Information and Event Management (SIEM) systems for real-time analysis. Machine learning-based anomaly detection can identify unusual authentication patterns, such as multiple failed login attempts from different geographic locations, helping security teams detect and respond to potential threats.

Organizations integrating SSO with mobile and IoT devices must adopt a multi-layered security approach combining OAuth 2.0-based authentication, biometric security, certificate-based IoT authentication, and continuous risk evaluation. By leveraging modern identity standards, secure token storage, and adaptive authentication policies, they can achieve a balance between seamless user experience and strong security controls.

Cross-Domain Identity Federation: Challenges and Solutions

Cross-domain identity federation enables secure authentication and authorization across multiple organizations, business entities, or government agencies, allowing users to access resources in different security domains without maintaining separate credentials. This approach improves user experience, security, and administrative efficiency, particularly in scenarios such as intergovernmental collaborations, business-to-business (B2B) integrations, cloud service access, and global enterprise identity management. However, cross-domain identity federation presents numerous challenges, including trust establishment, interoperability, security risks, regulatory compliance, and identity synchronization. Addressing these challenges requires a combination of standardized protocols, security best practices, and robust identity governance frameworks.

One of the primary challenges in cross-domain federation is establishing and maintaining trust between identity providers (IdPs) and service providers (SPs) across different domains. Unlike traditional single-organization identity federation, where trust is managed internally, cross-domain federation requires formal agreements and technical integration between separate entities. Organizations must define mutual authentication policies, encryption standards, and certificate management procedures to ensure secure authentication transactions. Federated trust can be established using bilateral agreements (one-to-one federation) or multilateral federation models, where multiple organizations rely on a trusted third-party federation hub.

Interoperability issues also pose significant challenges in cross-domain federation. Different organizations may use incompatible identity management systems, authentication protocols, and attribute schemas. Common identity federation protocols such as SAML (Security Assertion Markup Language), OpenID Connect (OIDC), and OAuth 2.0 help bridge these gaps by providing standardized authentication and authorization mechanisms. However, variations in identity attribute formats, role mappings, and policy enforcement can create inconsistencies. Organizations must implement identity normalization strategies, ensuring that attributes exchanged between domains follow a standardized schema to maintain consistent access control policies.

Security concerns in cross-domain federation include authentication assertion integrity, token replay prevention, session hijacking risks, and insider threats. Since authentication assertions and access tokens travel across different security domains, attackers may attempt to intercept or manipulate authentication data. To mitigate these risks, organizations should enforce digital signature verification, token encryption, and secure transport mechanisms (TLS 1.2 or higher). Additionally, mutual TLS (mTLS) can be used to validate both the requesting entity and the responding identity provider, preventing unauthorized actors from impersonating legitimate federation participants.

Another major challenge is identity lifecycle management across federated domains. When a user's employment status changes, their access rights must be updated or revoked across all federated systems. However, cross-domain federation complicates user deprovisioning, as identity providers and service providers operate under separate administrative controls. To address this, organizations use System for Cross-domain Identity Management (SCIM), an open standard for automating user provisioning, attribute synchronization, and account deactivation across federated domains. SCIM ensures that when a user is added, updated, or removed in one domain, these changes propagate consistently to all federated entities.

Regulatory and compliance requirements add another layer of complexity to cross-domain federation. Different organizations may be subject to industry-specific or region-specific regulations, such as GDPR (General Data Protection Regulation), HIPAA (Health Insurance Portability and Accountability Act), and NIST 800-63 digital identity guidelines. Compliance challenges arise when identity attributes contain personally identifiable information (PII) that must be protected according to data sovereignty laws. Organizations must implement data minimization strategies, ensuring that only necessary identity attributes are shared, and leverage pseudonymization techniques to protect user privacy.

Role-based and attribute-based access control (RBAC/ABAC) integration is another critical consideration in cross-domain federation. Since different organizations have varying role definitions, permission models, and access policies, federated access control must account for role mapping inconsistencies. An employee in one organization with a Manager role might not have the same privileges as a user with the Manager role in another domain. To resolve this, organizations implement attribute-based access control (ABAC) policies that dynamically evaluate user attributes, risk levels, and contextual conditions before granting access to federated resources.

Authentication assurance levels and step-up authentication are also key concerns. Some federated applications require higher security standards, such as multi-factor authentication (MFA) or risk-based authentication, while others operate with lower security thresholds. A federated user attempting to access a high-security system may need to undergo step-up authentication, where additional verification (e.g., biometric authentication, security tokens) is required before access is granted. Organizations implement risk-based authentication policies that dynamically assess authentication assurance levels and trigger step-up authentication when necessary.

Cross-domain federation in cloud environments introduces additional challenges. Organizations federating identities across multiple cloud service providers (e.g., AWS, Microsoft Azure, Google Cloud) must integrate cloud identity federation solutions such as Azure AD B2B, AWS IAM Identity Center, and Google Workspace Federation. These services enable secure authentication for cloud applications while maintaining centralized identity governance. However, organizations must also enforce consistent security policies across cloud platforms, ensuring that access controls and authentication mechanisms align with internal security requirements.

Federation governance and auditing are essential for maintaining security in cross-domain identity federation. Since multiple organizations share authentication responsibilities, federation agreements must define clear policies on authentication logging, auditing, and incident response. Federated systems should integrate with Security Information and Event Management (SIEM) solutions, allowing organizations to monitor authentication events, detect anomalies, and investigate security incidents across federated domains.

One approach to simplifying cross-domain federation is leveraging federation hubs and identity brokers, which act as intermediaries between different identity providers and service providers. Instead of establishing direct trust relationships between each federated entity, organizations connect to a central federation hub, which handles authentication requests and enforces standardized policies. Examples of such federation frameworks include eduGAIN for academic institutions, InCommon Federation for research organizations, and the U.S. Federal Identity, Credential, and Access Management (FICAM) framework for government entities.

Organizations implementing cross-domain identity federation must also plan for business continuity and failover mechanisms. If an identity provider in a federated system experiences downtime or service disruptions, users may be unable to authenticate, impacting critical operations. To address this, organizations deploy redundant IdPs, failover authentication mechanisms, and cached authentication assertions, ensuring high availability and resilience in federated identity environments.

Cross-domain identity federation plays a crucial role in modern digital ecosystems, enabling secure authentication, seamless user access, and enhanced collaboration across organizations, government agencies, and cloud providers. By addressing trust management, interoperability, security enforcement, compliance, and identity lifecycle challenges, organizations can successfully implement scalable and secure federated identity frameworks.

Leveraging AI and Machine Learning in Identity Management

Artificial Intelligence (AI) and Machine Learning (ML) are transforming identity management, enabling organizations to enhance security, automate identity governance, and improve user authentication experiences. Traditional identity and access management (IAM) solutions rely on static policies and manual configurations, which can be slow to adapt to emerging threats. AI-driven identity management introduces adaptive authentication, anomaly detection, behavior-based access control, and real-time risk analysis, making it a crucial component of modern security architectures.

One of the most impactful applications of AI in identity management is adaptive authentication. Traditional authentication mechanisms rely on fixed rules, such as requiring users to log in with passwords and multi-factor authentication (MFA) at predefined intervals. AI-based authentication systems analyze real-time contextual data, such as device type, location, login history, and behavioral patterns, to determine the level of authentication required. For example, if a user logs in from a recognized device and location, the system may allow access with minimal authentication friction. However, if the login request originates from an unusual location or device, the system may trigger step-up authentication, requiring additional verification such as a one-time passcode (OTP) or biometric authentication.

AI-powered anomaly detection is another major advancement in identity management. Traditional IAM systems rely on predefined security policies that may not detect sophisticated cyber threats. Machine learning models continuously analyze authentication logs, access patterns, and user behavior to detect suspicious activities that may indicate compromised accounts, insider threats, or brute-force attacks. These systems can identify unusual login attempts, unauthorized privilege escalations, and sudden access pattern deviations, alerting security teams in real time.

For example, if an employee typically logs in from New York at 9 AM using a corporate-issued laptop but suddenly attempts to log in from another country at 3 AM using an unknown device, an AI-driven IAM system can flag this as a potential security incident. Instead of allowing the login, the system can block access, request identity verification, or escalate the incident to security teams for investigation.

Behavioral biometrics further enhances identity security by leveraging AI to analyze how users interact with systems. Unlike traditional biometric authentication, which relies on fingerprints or facial recognition, behavioral biometrics examines typing speed, mouse movement patterns, touch gestures, and navigation habits to create a unique user profile. If an attacker gains access to a valid username and password but exhibits an unusual typing rhythm or interaction pattern, the system can flag the session as suspicious and trigger additional security measures.

AI also plays a critical role in privileged access management (PAM) by continuously monitoring privileged accounts and administrator activities. Privileged accounts, such as system administrators, database managers, and cloud security engineers, have elevated access to critical infrastructure, making them a prime target for cyberattacks. AI-driven PAM solutions analyze session recordings, command-line inputs, and access logs to detect potential misuse of privileged credentials. If an administrator attempts to execute an unusual command or access a restricted system, AI can automatically enforce security policies, blocking the action or alerting security teams.

Identity lifecycle automation is another key benefit of AI-driven identity management. Traditional IAM systems require manual provisioning and deprovisioning of user accounts, which can lead to delays, security gaps, and excessive permissions. AI-driven identity governance automates user onboarding, access changes, and account termination, ensuring that users only retain necessary privileges. When an employee changes roles, moves to another department, or leaves the organization, AI can analyze access patterns and role requirements to automatically adjust permissions, reducing the risk of orphaned accounts or excessive privileges.

AI and ML also improve role-based access control (RBAC) and attribute-based access control (ABAC) by dynamically adjusting access policies based on real-time risk analysis. Traditional RBAC models rely on static roles, which may not adapt to evolving security threats or business needs. AI-driven access control systems analyze historical access data, job functions, and security trends to recommend fine-grained access permissions. If an employee rarely accesses a specific application, AI can suggest revoking unnecessary permissions, improving security while reducing administrative overhead.

In federated identity environments, AI-driven solutions enhance cross-domain authentication and trust evaluation. Organizations participating in identity federation must assess the security posture of identity providers (IdPs) and service providers (SPs) to prevent trust exploitation. AI can analyze federated authentication logs, access policies, and identity reputation scores to determine whether a federated partner is exhibiting abnormal authentication behaviors. If an IdP is compromised or issuing anomalous authentication requests, AI-driven threat intelligence can detect these anomalies and dynamically restrict access.

Fraud detection and identity verification benefit significantly from AI and ML technologies. AI-powered identity verification solutions use computer vision, natural language processing (NLP), and document analysis to validate government-issued IDs, passports, and biometric data. This is particularly useful in remote onboarding scenarios, where organizations must verify the identity of new users without in-person verification. AI-driven fraud detection systems analyze user behavior, transaction history, and device intelligence to identify synthetic identities, fraudulent account takeovers, and deepfake-based identity spoofing.

AI also enhances passwordless authentication, reducing reliance on traditional credentials, which are often vulnerable to phishing and credential-stuffing attacks. Organizations are increasingly adopting passwordless authentication methods, such as biometric logins, security keys (FIDO2), and adaptive authentication, where AI dynamically assesses risk factors to determine whether additional verification is needed. This reduces the attack surface while improving user convenience.

Despite its advantages, AI-driven identity management presents challenges such as bias in AI models, false positives, and data privacy concerns. If an AI system incorrectly flags legitimate authentication attempts as fraudulent, it can disrupt user access and create operational inefficiencies. Organizations must continuously train and refine AI models, ensuring they balance security with user experience. Additionally, AI-based IAM solutions must comply with data privacy regulations such as GDPR, CCPA, and ISO 27001, ensuring that AI-driven decisions do not unintentionally violate user privacy rights.

AI and machine learning are revolutionizing identity management, enabling adaptive security, intelligent threat detection, automated identity governance, and dynamic access control. By integrating AI-powered identity solutions, organizations can enhance security while ensuring a seamless, efficient authentication experience for users across cloud, mobile, and enterprise environments.

Decentralized Identity and Self-Sovereign Identity (SSI)

Decentralized identity and Self-Sovereign Identity (SSI) are transforming digital identity management by shifting control over personal identity from centralized authorities to individual users. Traditional identity systems rely on third-party identity providers (IdPs) such as governments, enterprises, or social platforms to verify and store user identities. However, these centralized models create privacy concerns, security risks, and reliance on external organizations for authentication. In contrast, decentralized identity frameworks leverage blockchain, cryptographic credentials, and distributed ledgers to enable users to manage and control their own digital identities without requiring a centralized authority.

At the core of decentralized identity is the concept of user ownership and control over identity data. Instead of an organization holding a user's personal details in a database, the user stores their identity credentials in a digital wallet on their device. These credentials can include government-issued IDs, academic certificates, employment history, or healthcare records. When a user needs to authenticate or prove their identity, they present verifiable credentials, which can be cryptographically validated by relying parties without the need to contact the issuing authority.

A fundamental technology enabling decentralized identity is blockchain and distributed ledger technology (DLT). Unlike centralized identity systems where identity providers maintain authentication records, decentralized identity systems use public-key cryptography and decentralized identifiers (DIDs) stored on a blockchain. A DID is a unique, self-generated identifier that does not rely on a central registry. Users create their own DIDs and associated cryptographic keys, ensuring they have sole control over their identity. DIDs are immutable and can be verified without relying on a third party, making them resistant to identity theft and unauthorized modifications.

Verifiable credentials (VCs) play a crucial role in Self-Sovereign Identity. These are digitally signed identity claims that users can present to organizations without exposing unnecessary personal data. For example, a university may issue a verifiable credential for a degree certificate, and the holder can present it to an employer. The employer can then verify its authenticity using the university's public cryptographic key, without needing to query the university directly. This model enhances privacy by reducing the need for continuous interactions between identity issuers and verifiers.

One of the key advantages of SSI is selective disclosure, where users can choose which identity attributes to share based on the verification requirements. For example, instead of presenting a full government ID to prove they are over 18, a user can share only the age verification credential without revealing other personal details such as name, address, or ID number. This concept, known as zero-knowledge proofs (ZKPs), enhances privacy while ensuring compliance with identity verification policies.

Decentralized identity also improves security and resistance to identity fraud. Traditional identity systems are vulnerable to data breaches, as they store vast amounts of user credentials in centralized databases. If a central identity provider is compromised, millions of user records may be exposed. In contrast, decentralized identity eliminates central identity stores, reducing the risk of mass data leaks. Since users manage their own credentials and authentication is based on cryptographic proofs, attackers cannot steal or forge identities from a single point of failure.

Another significant benefit of SSI is interoperability and portability. Traditional identity systems create walled gardens, where users must create separate credentials for each platform or service. SSI allows users to carry their verifiable credentials across different services, platforms, and countries without re-registering. For example, a decentralized healthcare credential issued in one country can be used to access medical services in another country, provided the service provider supports the same SSI standard.

Decentralized identity frameworks rely on open standards and protocols such as W3C Decentralized Identifiers (DIDs), W3C Verifiable Credentials (VCs), and the DIDComm messaging protocol. These standards enable interoperability between identity wallets, verification services, and credential issuers, ensuring that decentralized identity solutions can be widely adopted across industries. Organizations such as Sovrin, Hyperledger Indy, Microsoft Entra Verified ID, and the European Blockchain Services Infrastructure (EBSI) are actively developing SSI solutions that comply with these standards.

Despite its advantages, decentralized identity faces several challenges and adoption barriers. One of the biggest obstacles is lack of widespread infrastructure and adoption. Many organizations and governments still rely on centralized identity providers, making it difficult for users to find services that accept verifiable credentials. Additionally, the onboarding process for SSI users can be complex, requiring users to understand concepts such as private key management, blockchain transactions, and credential revocation.

Another challenge is key management and account recovery. Since SSI eliminates centralized control, users are responsible for storing and protecting their private keys. If a user loses their cryptographic keys or access to their digital identity wallet, they may lose control over their credentials permanently. To address this, solutions such as social recovery mechanisms, multi-signature authentication, and decentralized backup methods are being developed to provide users with secure recovery options.

Regulatory and compliance concerns also impact SSI adoption. Governments and enterprises must ensure decentralized identity solutions comply with data protection regulations such as GDPR, CCPA, and eIDAS. While SSI enhances privacy by reducing data collection, organizations need legal frameworks to determine liability, identity assurance levels, and credential validity periods. Some governments are exploring hybrid identity models, where decentralized credentials work alongside existing national identity systems to provide a balance between user control and regulatory compliance.

Decentralized identity also introduces challenges for fraud detection and risk assessment. Traditional identity providers use centralized logs and monitoring tools to track authentication patterns, suspicious activity, and account takeovers. In decentralized systems, identity transactions occur peer-to-peer, limiting visibility into fraudulent behavior and identity misuse. Organizations must develop decentralized risk assessment frameworks, leveraging AI-driven identity analytics, decentralized reputation systems, and trusted verification registries to combat fraud effectively.

Industries such as finance, healthcare, education, and government services are beginning to explore SSI as a way to improve trust, security, and user autonomy. Financial institutions can use decentralized KYC (Know Your Customer) processes, allowing users to verify their identity without repeatedly submitting documents to multiple banks. Universities can issue verifiable diplomas, reducing credential fraud in job applications. Governments can provide digital identity wallets for citizens, enabling secure and private access to public services.

Decentralized identity and Self-Sovereign Identity (SSI) represent a shift towards user-centric digital identity, reducing reliance on centralized identity providers while enhancing privacy, security, and interoperability. As organizations adopt blockchain-based identity frameworks, verifiable credentials, and decentralized authentication models, users gain greater control over their digital identities, transforming the way authentication and identity verification are conducted across industries.

Using Microsoft Entra ID (Azure AD) for Federated Identity

Microsoft Entra ID, formerly known as Azure Active Directory (Azure AD), is a cloud-based identity and access management (IAM) service that enables federated identity across cloud and on-premises environments. Organizations use Entra ID to provide secure authentication, Single Sign-On (SSO), and access control across Microsoft 365, third-party SaaS applications, hybrid infrastructures, and multi-cloud deployments. By leveraging identity federation, businesses can eliminate password sprawl, improve security posture, and simplify user access management across multiple domains.

At the core of federated identity with Microsoft Entra ID is the ability to establish trust relationships between identity providers (IdPs) and service providers (SPs). Entra ID supports Security Assertion Markup Language (SAML), OpenID Connect (OIDC), OAuth 2.0, and WS-Federation, allowing organizations to federate identities with third-party applications, business partners, and external authentication providers. This federation capability ensures that users can authenticate once and seamlessly access multiple applications without needing to re-enter credentials.

One of the most common use cases for federated identity in Microsoft Entra ID is hybrid identity integration. Many organizations operate in a hybrid IT environment, where they maintain on-premises Active Directory (AD) infrastructure while leveraging cloud-based applications. Entra ID enables hybrid identity through Azure AD Connect, a synchronization tool that links on-prem AD user accounts with cloud-based identities. This setup allows employees to sign in with their existing credentials while enforcing consistent authentication policies across on-prem and cloud applications.

Single Sign-On (SSO) with Entra ID is a fundamental component of federated identity. Organizations can configure federated SSO with Microsoft 365, enterprise SaaS applications, and custom line-of-business applications. Entra ID supports password-based SSO, federated SSO, and pass-through authentication (PTA), allowing businesses to choose an authentication model that fits their security requirements. With federated SSO, users authenticate through a central identity provider (such as an on-prem AD FS server or third-party IdP), and Entra ID issues authentication tokens that grant access to federated services.

For organizations that require federation with external identity providers, Microsoft Entra ID supports direct federation, allowing users to authenticate using third-party IdPs such as Okta, Ping Identity, or Google Workspace. This is particularly useful in mergers and acquisitions, B2B collaborations, and multi-cloud identity federation scenarios, where users need seamless authentication across different identity ecosystems. Entra ID allows organizations to define custom federation policies, ensuring that authentication requests follow strict security and access control guidelines.

Conditional Access policies in federated authentication allow organizations to enforce risk-based authentication and access controls. Microsoft Entra ID enables adaptive authentication based on user risk, device security posture, and network conditions. For example, if a federated user attempts to sign in from an unfamiliar IP address or an untrusted device, the system can trigger multi-factor authentication (MFA) or deny access based on security policies. Organizations can define location-based, device-based, or session-based access policies, ensuring that federated authentication aligns with zero trust security principles.

Multi-factor authentication (MFA) and passwordless authentication are crucial for securing federated identities. Microsoft Entra ID integrates Azure MFA, allowing organizations to require additional authentication factors, such as one-time passcodes, biometric verification, or FIDO2 security keys, for high-risk authentication scenarios. Entra ID also supports passwordless authentication methods such as Windows Hello for Business, Microsoft Authenticator App, and hardware security keys, reducing reliance on passwords while improving authentication security.

Another significant use case for Microsoft Entra ID is B2B and B2C identity federation. With Microsoft Entra External ID, organizations can establish federated authentication for external partners, contractors, and customers. Businesses can invite guest users to collaborate securely using federated authentication with their home identity providers. This is especially useful in partner ecosystems, supplier networks, and customer-facing applications, where external users need controlled access to internal resources without creating duplicate accounts.

Microsoft Entra ID B2B collaboration allows organizations to use federated authentication with external identity providers, reducing administrative overhead while ensuring consistent access governance. External users can authenticate using their corporate credentials from Google Workspace, Okta, Active Directory Federation Services (AD FS), or any SAML/OIDC-compatible IdP. This enables businesses to extend their identity perimeter securely without managing separate identity stores for external partners.

In addition to traditional federation scenarios, Microsoft Entra ID integrates with multi-cloud identity architectures, enabling organizations to manage federated authentication across AWS, Google Cloud, and on-prem data centers. By configuring federated SSO with third-party cloud providers, organizations can ensure that employees, contractors, and cloud workloads authenticate through a centralized identity management framework.

Security in federated identity is a primary concern, and Microsoft Entra ID offers advanced identity protection features such as Identity Protection and Privileged Identity Management (PIM). Identity Protection uses machine learning algorithms to detect anomalous authentication attempts, impossible travel logins, and leaked credentials, allowing administrators to enforce automated remediation actions. Privileged Identity Management (PIM) enhances federated access security by allowing organizations to enforce just-in-time (JIT) privileged access, ensuring that high-risk accounts only receive elevated permissions for a limited time.

Federated identity governance is another key aspect of using Microsoft Entra ID. Organizations must ensure that federated authentication aligns with compliance frameworks such as GDPR, HIPAA, ISO 27001, and SOC 2. Entra ID integrates with Microsoft Identity Governance, providing automated access reviews, role assignments, and policy enforcement across federated applications. By leveraging Identity Governance workflows, administrators can define policies that automatically grant, review, or revoke federated access based on user role changes, employment status, or compliance requirements.

Microsoft Entra ID also provides logging and monitoring capabilities for federated authentication events. Organizations can integrate Azure AD logs with Microsoft Sentinel (SIEM) to track authentication attempts, failed login events, and security alerts. This enhances incident detection and response, allowing security teams to detect compromised federated accounts, investigate suspicious access patterns, and implement risk mitigation strategies.

As organizations continue to adopt cloud-first and hybrid identity strategies, Microsoft Entra ID remains a leading identity federation platform for enabling secure, scalable authentication across cloud, hybrid, and multi-domain environments. By leveraging federated SSO, conditional access policies, multi-cloud federation, and zero trust identity models, businesses can ensure seamless user authentication while enforcing strong security controls.

www.ingramcontent.com/pod-product-compliance
Lightning Source LLC
LaVergne TN
LVHW051245050326
832903LV00028B/2571